RSAC

T5-AQQ-485

2012

Small Adventures in Cooking

James Ramsden

Small Adventures in Cooking

James Ramsden

Photography by Steven Joyce

LYONS PRESS
Guilford, Connecticut
An imprint of Globe Pequot Press

For my sister, Mary, the greatest and greediest roommate a brother could hope for.

To buy books in quantity for corporate use
or incentives, call **(800) 962-0973**
or e-mail **premiums@GlobePequot.com.**

Text © 2011 James Ramsden
Photography © 2011 Steven Joyce
Design and layout © 2011 Quadrille Publishing Ltd

First published in 2011 by Quadrille Publishing Limited

First published in the United States in 2012 by Lyons Press

ALL RIGHTS RESERVED. No part of this book may be reproduced or transmitted in any form by any means, electronic or mechanical, including photocopying and recording, or by any information storage and retrieval system, except as may be expressly permitted in writing from the publisher. Requests for permission should be addressed to Globe Pequot Press, Attn: Rights and Permissions Department, P.O. Box 480, Guilford, CT 06437.

Lyons Press is an imprint of Globe Pequot Press

Library of Congress Cataloging-in-Publication Data is available on file.

ISBN 978-0-7627-8020-4

Printed in China

10 9 8 7 6 5 4 3 2 1

Introduction

I believe in fuss-free food. Cooking that demands 18 different processes, 12 saucepans, and an assemblage of utensils makes me want to seek refuge under a blanket. It's time-consuming, messy, and often traumatic—when you aim that high, the end result is almost always going to disappoint. It is cooking that is best left to professionals and wannabes.

Surely the kitchen should be a place of comfort and reassurance, not terror and torment—a place where, at the end of a long day, you unwind, play some music, have a drink, and get stuck into some cooking. I find it an ideal time to get lost in my thoughts. Humdrum jobs such as peeling potatoes, washing salads, or podding peas become opportunities for involuntary meditation. Your mind wanders, the day is processed, problems are solved, and you soon realize you've been peeling the same potato for ten minutes.

But as with many things in life, the potentially mundane task of cooking can be transformed into a joy if it is approached with a sense of adventure. I'm not talking about crossing continents or ingesting insects, but just about lifting it beyond the everyday. Once you have even the most basic grasp of cooking it doesn't take much to make it a great deal more compelling.

If you tend to shop at the supermarket, then just heading to a butcher, fishmonger, or ethnic store might feel like an adventure. Investigating the various seasonal vegetables at the local farmers' market or asking the grocer about his favorite way to cook celery root help make food that little bit more interesting, more personal.

It would be impractical and unrealistic to suggest doing this every day, but the odd bit of novelty is rewarding— nothing wildly ambitious or laborious or expensive; just enough to break the routine and generate an air of excitement in the kitchen. Because, devoid of adventure, cooking can be a pain. With it, on the other hand, cooking will keep you amused and the frozen dinners at bay.

I chose these recipes because I think each one kindles a little of that adventurous spirit without being overly technical or complex. Some can be knocked out one-handed while chatting on the phone. Others require a little more finesse. All are suitable for cooks of any ability.

So come and join me on a small culinary adventure of fast feasts, swanky suppers, lazy brunches, and late-night munchies. Let's set the compass, fire up the engine, and sail beyond our culinary comfort zone.

A few things to take on board

Have a loose agenda

Few things make food as loveless and perfunctory as a fixed-in-granite shopping list. To shop with blinders on is to miss out on so much opportunity—you're only a sucker for special deals if you buy what you don't need and won't use. Come home from the grocery store with two bags of salad and a half-price box of pancakes and you have indeed fallen for their cunning ploys. But pragmatically purchase something new and exciting that intrigues you, and you are already one step closer to making your cooking into more of an adventure.

By all means take a list—if only to avoid the tedium of realizing you forgot to buy garbage bags and toilet paper—but do be aware that flexible planning makes the shopping and the cooking more fun. *See p.29 for my shopping tips.*

Keep an ear to the ground

People love to talk about food. From the strange Polish man with a penchant for potatoes who introduced me to canned sorrel (a video of which is on my blog), to the drunk in the local bar who spent an entire hour talking me through his recipe for Pheasant Picardy, it's common ground for everyone, and people enjoy offering an opinion. As well as making for great entertainment, such discussions are inspiring reminders that there are very few absolutes in cooking. In fact, there are hundreds of ways of doing everything—therein lies the fun. Sticking to one method gets boring very quickly, so see what you find out next time you ask the person at the checkout how they roast a chicken. *See p.57 for tips on engaging conversation with shopkeepers.*

Make your itinerary flexible

To follow a recipe religiously is to be manacled to your stove-top, a slave to culinary cartography. If Columbus had had a half-decent map and stuck to it, he never would have found America. Tweak and tinker; if something sounds wrong to you, change it. If you're missing an ingredient, try out an alternative. Very few things are set in stone. *See p.71 for tips on tweaking.*

Trust your instincts

Even if you are lacking in confidence, your gut will most likely let you know if something is right or wrong. If a recipe calls for two tablespoons of ground cumin but a little voice in your ear is telling you that sounds like a lot, then you're probably right. Call friends or look online if you're not sure about something. *See p.151 for tips on tasting and seasoning.*

Make a battle plan

This isn't a military exercise, but if you're to pull off a dish then you do need some plan of attack. Not one to stick to immovably (see above), but a good idea of where you're heading. Think of it as a plan on which to improvise. Work out what you need, get the things that require chopping, slicing, washing, or measuring chopped, sliced, washed, and measured. Take your time—food rarely needs cooking in one sitting—and when you're ready, off you go. *See p.135 for prepping tips.*

Keep a karma kitchen

Wash up as you go. "Boring!" I hear you cry. Perhaps, but not nearly as boring, tiresome, and panic-inducing as trying to cook on two square inches of work surface while the rest of the kitchen looks like the washup in a Siberian prison. Embrace it as part of the deal, stick on some music, and enjoy it. Cooking is more relaxing in a clean and tidy kitchen. *See p.113 for tips on keeping a clean kitchen.*

Have a sense of humor

There isn't a cook alive who doesn't make mistakes on a regular basis. From basic mistakes like overseasoning to great big whoppers like dropping a pot of stew for 20 people, these things happen. As Edison put it, you haven't failed, you've found a way that doesn't work. Console yourself with the fact that later you'll be laughing about it. *See p.171 for thoughts on messing up.*

A couple more things...

Hashtags

If you are a Twitter user then you can discuss the recipes in this book online. Each recipe has a hashtag beneath it (for example, "#cullenskink"), so you can tweet about the recipe, offering tips and tweaks to other users.

Getting in touch

You can email me with any queries or qualms: smalladventuresincooking@gmail.com
Or tweet me @jteramsden

Happy cooking!

James

Va va voyages

Va va voyages

It's not every night that we have the time or the patience to spend an hour moseying around the kitchen. There are those evenings when you want supper on the table within half an hour. While I'm not into imposing time limits on a dish—surely that takes all the fun out of cooking—all the recipes in this chapter materialize pretty much on target.

Some have a little leeway, or a nifty shortcut, so that if you are in a rush you can have dinner ready chop-chop. Others give a little temporal wiggle room, so that if you want to put the supper on and then go and have a bath, you can. These are recipes to take at your own pace. The last thing you want at the end of a nightmarish day is to be galloping around the kitchen, fettered by the implication that if you don't finish cooking by the time your keys have stopped swinging on the hook, then you have somehow failed.

Most importantly, "quick and simple" should never have to mean "predictable and dull." The impetus to cook on a weeknight is always going to be much greater if the end product is something exciting and novel, and I think these dishes provide that sense of express adventure.

All of the following recipes serve two. They can be simply multiplied (and indeed halved), so that should there be last-minute dinner guests, you can adapt easily.

Roast butternut squash with taleggio, walnuts, and honey

There was a time when I couldn't be bothered with squash. This was largely down to them being a pain to peel. Unless you have a viciously sharp peeler you need to resort to using a knife, which you are liable to end up sticking in your wrist—a little too perilous for my liking. So imagine my joy when I discovered that there is absolutely no need to peel squash. When roasted, the skin goes pleasingly chewy, rather like garlic skin.

Serves 2

1 small butternut squash, scrubbed
a sprig of thyme, leaves picked
salt and pepper
olive oil
¾ ounce flat-leaf parsley, leaves only
a handful of shelled walnuts, roughly chopped
4 ounces Taleggio cheese
2 teaspoons runny honey

Preheat the oven to 400°F.
   Trim the squash and cut in half lengthwise. Scoop out the seeds and cut into thick wedges. Toss in the thyme leaves, salt, pepper, and a drizzle of olive oil and cook in the oven for 45 minutes.
   Serve with a scattering of parsley leaves and walnuts, slices of Taleggio, honey, and a drizzle of oil.

#roastsquashsalad

Tart—Well, you can tart this quite literally. Roast the squash as above, then place on some ready-rolled puff pastry, top with the Taleggio, and a drizzle of oil and put in the oven for 20 minutes at 350°F. Finish off with the walnuts, honey, and parsley.

Tweak—If you struggle to find Taleggio then you could use goat cheese instead, or try a soft French cheese like Munster.

Tomorrow—Roughly chop any leftovers and toss through couscous for a lovely salad.

Thai pork patties

Ground meat has a reputation as a boring fallback, a thrifty food for the unimaginative student or exhausted mother. But it's such a great base for messing about with flavors and seasonings—forgiving and receptive to all kinds of ingredients being thrown into it and mixed about.

Here the bread crumbs both bulk out the meat and absorb its juices, meaning flavor stays in the patties and doesn't end up in the pan. You can buy bread crumbs ready-made these days, but otherwise just get stale or ever-so-slightly toasted bread and finely chop or blend it.

Serves 2

12 ounces ground pork
a stalk of lemongrass, minced
1 fresh red chili, deseeded (see p.23) and minced
2 green onions, trimmed and sliced
a handful of cilantro, chopped
juice of ½ a lime
a small handful of bread crumbs
1 egg, beaten
salt and pepper
olive oil
a few Boston lettuce leaves
a few mint leaves
sweet chili sauce

Mix the ground pork, lemongrass, chili, onions, cilantro, lime juice, bread crumbs, and beaten egg together by hand. Season with salt and pepper and form into four medium-sized patties.

Heat a little oil over medium-high heat in a nonstick frying pan. Add the patties and fry for 4 minutes on each side. Remove from the pan and rest for a minute or two, then serve wrapped in Boston lettuce leaves with some torn mint and a good shake of sweet chili sauce.

#thaiporkpatties

Tart—Pork and ginger always go very well together, so try adding a tablespoon of grated ginger to the mixture. Or, you could sandwich the patty with a generous spoonful of the *kimchi* (pickled cabbage) on p.147 between two warm bun halves.

Tweak—Substitute the pork with ground beef or chicken.

Mushrooms on toast

When I was 19 I spent a hot summer cooking in the south of France. One day the previous cook came to stay and, on my day off, made lunch. He produced mushrooms on toast, and I remember being blown away at how something so seemingly drab and old-fashioned tasted so magnificent. I had to freshen up my ideas after that.

His trick was to cook the onions at a glacial pace with lots of butter. This version is quicker but doesn't, I don't think, suffer much from the speedier caramelization of the onions. The Marsala is optional but enhances the sweetness of the onions, as well as adding great depth of flavor.

Serves 2

2 tablespoons butter
1 onion, peeled and
  finely sliced
salt and pepper
a wineglass of Marsala
  (optional)
9 ounces button mushrooms,
  quartered
⅓ cup heavy cream
a small bunch of flat-leaf
  parsley, minced, plus extra
  for serving
juice of 1 lemon
2 slices of good bread
¾ ounce Parmesan cheese

Melt the butter in a frying pan over medium heat and add the onions. Season with salt and pepper and cook for 15 minutes, stirring regularly to avoid burning. (You can get away with less—7 or 8 minutes—if particularly hungry, but the longer you cook the onions, the more of the natural sugars you'll extract, and the richer they'll taste.)

Add the Marsala, if using, and simmer for a minute or two until slightly reduced. Now add the mushrooms and cream, cover, and simmer gently for 5 minutes, until the mushrooms have cooked through. Uncover and simmer for another 5–7 minutes, until the sauce has thickened. Remove from the heat and stir in the chopped parsley and lemon juice.

Toast the bread. Spoon the mushrooms over the toast, grate over the Parmesan, and scatter over a few parsley leaves. Serve.

#mushroomsontoast

⟹ TART—This would make a very good side dish for chicken. Try frying a couple of chicken breasts and serving on top of the mushrooms.

⟹ TWEAK—If you're not a fan of parsley (and many aren't), you can always substitute chives instead. A couple of teaspoons of finely sliced chives should do the trick.

⟹ TOMORROW—Leftover mushrooms work well tossed through pasta or used as the base for a soup.

Chicken and coconut noodle soup

Noodles have got to be among the greatest comfort foods around. When tired and famished on a Sunday night it's pasta I turn to: ribbons of pappardelle kissed by a creamy sausage sauce, or savory spaghetti with anchovy, chili, and garlic for a kick up the backside. When feeling delicate, though—stuffed up with cold or, more often than not, some self-inflicted malady—it is broth I yearn for. Soothing and fresh, it at once restores and invigorates.

Serves 2

peanut oil
a thumb-sized piece of ginger, peeled and grated
2 red chilies, deseeded (see p.23) and sliced
zest of 1 lime
stalks from a small bunch of cilantro, minced
a clove of garlic, crushed
2 cups chicken stock (homemade or good store-bought stuff)
1 x 14-ounce can of coconut milk
1 tablespoon fish sauce
2 chicken breasts, sliced
7 ounces ramen, soba, or rice noodles
1 green onion, washed and sliced at an angle
a handful of cilantro leaves, roughly chopped
½ lime, cut into wedges

Heat a little peanut oil in a saucepan over medium-high heat and add the ginger, chilies, lime zest, cilantro, and garlic. Stir constantly for a minute before adding the chicken stock, coconut milk, and fish sauce. Bring to a boil.

Lower the heat to a simmer, add the chicken, and poach for 5 minutes. Meanwhile, bring another pan of water to a boil and cook the noodles according to package instructions.

Divide the noodles between large bowls and spoon in the broth and chicken. Garnish with onion, cilantro, and a wedge of lime. Serve.

#chickennoodlebroth

TART—I like adding sugar snap peas to this soup after I have added the chicken. Carrot ribbons peeled with a vegetable peeler also work well, as do bean sprouts scattered over at the end.

TWEAK—Substitute beef strips or shrimp for the chicken. You could also make a vegetarian version by omitting the chicken, using vegetable stock, and bulking up with mushrooms.

The world's laziest chicken curry

Takeout curry is often a knee-jerk reaction when you can't be bothered to cook. This is quite a good solution—providing that spicy, nostril-clearing hit as quickly as a delivery and at a fraction of the price.

Serves 2

2 tablespoons good store-bought curry paste
2 tablespoons plain yogurt
juice of ½ a lemon
salt and pepper
2 whole chicken legs (the thigh and leg undivided)
½ cup basmati rice
scant 1 cup water

Preheat the oven to 375°F. Mix the curry paste, yogurt, and lemon juice together in a bowl, season with salt and pepper, and rub over the chicken. Bake in the oven for 45 minutes.

Meanwhile, put the rice and water in a saucepan and bring to a boil. Cover, turn down the heat, and simmer gently for 12 minutes. Don't peek—you need to keep the steam in there. Remove from the heat and leave for another 5 minutes, still not peeking. Uncover and leave for 2 minutes longer, before fluffing up with a fork. Serve with the curry.

#lazycurry

Tart—You could add chopped cilantro to the spice rub, or make a pilaf like the one on p.108 and a traditional raita (yogurt, chopped cucumber, and mint) to serve alongside.

Tweak—Swap the chicken pieces for a whole fish and roast for the same amount of time. Or put a sweet potato in the oven at the same time as the chicken in place of the rice.

A spicy beef salad with mushrooms

The idea of having salad for supper can smack of health hatches being battened down and short-lived Sunday night resolutions. But a good salad can be unbeatable when you feel like something light and fresh. The beef and the mushrooms here add depth and richness, but there's still enough sprightliness in the chilies and lime to keep this sufficiently light.

Serves 2

1–2 sirloin steaks (depending on hunger/size of steaks)
salt and pepper
olive oil
4½ cups sliced cremini or button mushrooms
½ a cucumber, cut into thin sticks
a handful of bean sprouts
½ a red onion, peeled and finely sliced
Boston lettuce leaves
a big handful of cilantro
a small handful of mint leaves

For the dressing

1 fresh red chili, deseeded (see opposite)
2 tablespoons peanut oil
juice of ½ a lime
½ teaspoon fish sauce
a few shakes of sesame oil
1 teaspoon soy sauce
a pinch of sugar

Make the salad dressing by finely slicing the chilies and mixing in a large bowl with the peanut oil, lime juice, fish sauce, sesame oil, soy sauce, and sugar. Set aside.

Season the steaks with salt and pepper and rub with olive oil. Get a frying pan smoking hot and fry for 2 minutes on each side. Remove to a plate to rest.

Add the mushrooms to the frying pan with a splash of olive oil. Fry until softened, then add to the bowl of dressing along with the cucumber, bean sprouts, onion, and lettuce leaves. Toss to dress, and arrange on a plate as you wish.

Slice the beef and lay on top, garnish with a few torn handfuls of cilantro and mint, and serve.

#beefsalad

Tart—Try using enoki mushrooms in place of the cremini or button mushrooms. They're East Asian mushrooms that look like they were harvested on some strange planet, but they have a lovely chestnut honey flavor when cooked.

Tweak—If you can't be bothered to slice up the mushrooms, you could always buy them ready-sliced.

✳ To deseed a chili

Cut the chili in half down
the middle and use the end of a
teaspoon to scrape out the seeds.
To get the oil from the chili
off your hands, rub them with
lemon juice before washing.

Lamb neck fillets with harissa and chickpea salad

This dish is pretty speedy stuff; just remember that you will need to get the lamb out of the refrigerator a good half-hour before cooking—essential unless you like your lamb tough and cold in the middle, not soft and pink. Consider it an opportunity to have a shower and put your feet up. The chickpea salad here is really a blank canvas—tart it up with whatever you want: crushed cumin seeds, chopped chilies, mint, feta ... go nuts. Harissa is a North African spice paste which can be found in specialty markets.

Serves 2

1 x 14-ounce can of chickpeas
salt and pepper
½ a red onion, peeled and minced
2 x 7-ounce lamb neck fillets, at room temperature
olive oil
2–3 teaspoons harissa (depending on how hot you like it)
a handful of cilantro leaves and stalks, roughly chopped or torn
juice of ½ a lemon
a dollop of plain yogurt

Drain and rinse the chickpeas. Place in a pan of salted water along with the red onion, bring to a boil, and simmer for 4 minutes. Drain and set aside.

Season the lamb generously with salt and pepper and rub with olive oil. Get a frying pan hot over medium-high heat, add the lamb, and cook for 6 or so minutes on each side, turning every couple of minutes to avoid burning. Remove to a plate to rest for 5 minutes.

Toss the harissa, cilantro, lemon juice, and yogurt through the chickpeas and season with salt and pepper.

Slice the lamb thickly and serve with the chickpea and harissa salad.

#lambneck

TART—If you've got more time, marinate the fillets in a little yogurt, ground cumin, chopped cilantro, and lemon juice for a couple of hours, before broiling or barbecuing.

TWEAK—If you're feeling rich, try using loin instead. The salad also works well with chicken.

TOMORROW—I'd definitely recommend doubling the quantities of the chickpea salad and taking the extra to work.

Broiled mackerel with zucchini ribbons and feta

Italians vehemently believe that fish and cheese shouldn't go together. For much Italian food this make sense; putting Parmesan cheese over a bowl of spaghetti and clams does feel a bit odd. But there are no absolutes with food and, although the Italians might turn their noses up at the idea, here they actually go very well together—the mild, chalky, salty feta sitting nicely alongside the fresh mackerel and acidic tang of the lemon juice.

Serves 2

3–4 medium zucchini
2 large or 4 small mackerel
  fillets
salt and pepper
olive oil
a handful of mint
a handful of raisins
4 ounces feta cheese,
  cut into chunks
juice of ½ a lemon

Preheat the broiler to as high as it will go. Using a vegetable peeler, peel the zucchini into thin strips. Set aside.

Season the mackerel with salt and pepper and rub with oil. Place under the broiler skin-side up, and cook for 5 minutes. (There's no need to turn them over.)

Meanwhile, heat a little oil in a frying pan and stir-fry the zucchini ribbons over high heat until soft and blistered. You may need to do this in batches. Remove from the heat and toss in the mint, raisins, and feta. Add the lemon juice, season with salt and pepper, and serve with the mackerel.

#grilledmackerel

Tart—Toast some pine nuts on the stove in a dry frying pan and scatter over the finished dish. They burn quite easily, so keep a close eye on them.

Tweak—For a summer lunch, substitute cucumber for the zucchini and omit the frying business.

Cullen skink

Cullen skink is as comforting as soups get. It's like a Scottish version of a chowder, but lighter than its American cousin, thanks to the absence of flour and the addition of wine. It's traditionally made using mashed potato, though I've opted for chunks here.

Serves 2

1 x 7-ounce fillet of undyed
  smoked haddock
scant 1 cup heavy cream
1¾ cups whole milk
1 bay leaf
olive oil
1 small onion, peeled
  and minced
a stalk of celery, trimmed and
  minced
1 large potato, cut into chunks
salt and pepper
a wineglass of white wine
a handful of flat-leaf parsley,
  chopped

Put the haddock, cream, and milk in a saucepan with the bay leaf. Place over medium heat, bring to a simmer, and cook gently for 5 minutes. (You may need to cut the fillet in half to fit, depending on the size of your saucepan.) Remove from the heat and let cool.

Heat a little olive oil in a separate saucepan and sweat the onion and celery until softened. Add the potato, season with salt and pepper to taste, cover, and cook for another 15 minutes, stirring occasionally. Meanwhile, take the fish out of the milk and remove the skin and any bones, flaking the fish as you go.

Throw a glass of wine over the potatoes, simmer for a minute or two, then add the cream and milk. Cook very gently, until the potato is completely soft, then add the fish flakes. Cook for a few more minutes, check for seasoning, scatter with chopped parsley, and serve with some good bread for moppage.

#cullenskink

TART—You could add some mussels along with the fish at the end of cooking. Cover for 3–5 minutes until they've opened. Add a can of corn for a twist.

TWEAK—If you're watching the paunch you could omit the cream and use all whole milk, mashing the potatoes before adding the fish to create the necessary thickness.

TOMORROW—This will keep in the refrigerator for a couple of days and can be reheated for lunch. Or breakfast. Or whatever.

Jerusalem artichoke and chorizo omelet

This is more akin to a Spanish omelet or tortilla, in that it contains starch and is fired under a broiler, as opposed to being folded over like the French version. The aim is to have your omelet set both top and bottom, but to be ever-so-slightly soft and runny in the middle.

Serves 2

2–3 Jerusalem artichokes, peeled and sliced about ½ inch thick
salt and pepper
olive oil
2 red onions, peeled and very roughly chopped
5 ounces spicy chorizo, cut into chunks
6 eggs
1 tablespoon whole milk
¼ cup grated manchego cheese

Preheat the broiler to high.

Bring the artichokes to a boil in a pan of lightly salted water and simmer for 5–7 minutes, until soft. Drain and let dry for a minute or two.

Meanwhile, add a good glug of olive oil to a frying pan and fry the onions over medium-high heat, stirring regularly, until soft and a little crisp at the edges. Add the artichoke and chorizo and fry until both are starting to color.

Beat the eggs in a bowl with a splash of milk and season with salt and pepper. Add to the pan and fry for a minute or two, until the base is set. Scatter the cheese on top and place under the broiler for 3 minutes before serving in wedges.

#spanishomelette

Tart—Where to start? I love adding those jarred red peppers you find in the grocery store, or you could toss in some jalapenos to give it that little extra kick.

Tweak—If you can't find Jerusalem artichokes, then you could always use baby potatoes. For a vegetarian version, use roasted red bell peppers instead of chorizo, and if you can't find manchego, then Parmesan or even cheddar works well, too.

Tomorrow—This is very nice cold for lunch the next day, or cut into chunks and served as a nibble before supper.

Va va voyages

Some shopping tips...

Surprise yourself

Don't feel too restricted by your shopping list. It's good to take one, but just as important to keep an open mind. I believe home cooks can gain more from an experimental attitude than an exhaustive knowledge. Cooking-by-numbers leaves no room for personalization or discovery, so if you see something new or interesting that intrigues you, give it a shot. Sometimes it's those colors and smells that give you the inspiration to cook, not a few scribbles on a piece of paper.

Top shelf vs. bottom shelf

There are times when it's worth spending a bit extra for a high-quality product, and times when it's not. Think about what you're using the ingredient for. If you're using eggs for baking then there's no need to go for the best eggs in the store, whereas if you're hoping to have a top-notch omelet then you're better off spending an extra dollar or two. A friend of mine used to transfer organic eggs into the cheap packs, but that's not recommended. Or, indeed, legal.

With canned food you're fine with the cheap stuff if it's playing a supporting role—say, a can of tomatoes in a Bolognese—though less so if it's more prominent. Vegetables that will be served as a side dish should be the best you can find, while if they're the base for a stew then you can compromise a little. You get the idea.

Special deals

We're often warned not to fall for the wicked ruses of store specials, which strikes me as a little cynical. Cherry-pick the right ones and you'll end up saving a fortune. Sure, if you buy two cartons of luxury orange juice for a negligible saving then you may be being somewhat gullible. But often you'll find a bargain. Canned goods and other things that keep well are always worth stocking up on, and if you have a decent-sized freezer then don't turn your nose up at reduced-price meat. You often find meat and fish heavily discounted at the very end of the day, when stringent regulations mean that stores have to get rid of perfectly good produce.

Tomato and goat cheese gratin

I love this dish both for its simplicity and its quirkiness. It's an adaptation of a recipe by Rory O'Connell of the Ballymaloe Cookery School in Ireland, and a dish that demonstrates how even with a few simple ingredients you can make something delicious and soothing but also different, too. It works as a light lunch or supper, or as a nifty little appetizer. If you don't have any ramekins, use sturdy mugs instead.

Serves 2

1½ tablespoons butter
1 shallot, peeled and minced
salt and pepper
2 large tomatoes or
  1 x 7-ounce can of good-
  quality diced tomatoes
a clove of garlic, peeled
  and minced
1 teaspoon sugar
1 tablespoon red-wine vinegar
a sprig of thyme
½ cup soft goat cheese
a pinch of dried mixed herbs
olive oil

Preheat the broiler as high as it will go.

Melt the butter in a saucepan over low heat and add the shallot. Season with salt and pepper and gently sweat until soft and translucent. Meanwhile, peel, deseed, and roughly chop the tomatoes (see opposite) before adding them with the garlic, sugar, vinegar, and thyme. Cover tightly and cook over medium heat for 10 minutes. Remove the lid and simmer for another 5 minutes, stirring occasionally, until slightly thickened.

Remove the sprig of thyme and divide the thickened sauce between individual ramekins. Crumble the goat cheese over the top, season with pepper and mixed herbs, drizzle with oil, and put under the broiler for 5–10 minutes, until golden and bubbling. Serve with toast.

#tomgoatcheese

TART—The tomato sauce can be perked up with the addition of chilies, chorizo, or basil.

TWEAK—Beets and goat cheese are a match made in heaven. Try replacing the tomato sauce with some boiled or ready-cooked beets, sliced and tossed through with balsamic vinegar and olive oil.

TOMORROW—This is lovely cold to take to work or on a picnic.

To peel a tomato

Boil water in a kettle. Meanwhile, make a cross in the bottom of each tomato with a sharp knife. Pour the boiling water over the tomatoes and let sit for a minute. Remove with a slotted spoon and cool, before pulling the skin off.

To deseed a tomato

Simply quarter and cut out the seeds with a knife or a teaspoon.

Broiled figs with crème fraîche and pistachios

The beauty of this dessert is that if, when the time comes, you're not in the mood for it, you can always have it for breakfast the next morning instead. Flexible dining or what?

Serves 2

2–4 figs (depending on size/hunger)
2 tablespoons light brown or Demerara sugar
4 teaspoons crème fraîche or plain yogurt
2 teaspoons runny honey
a small handful of pistachios, shelled and roughly chopped

Preheat the broiler to high.

Halve the figs down the middle lengthwise, sprinkle the cut sides with sugar, and place under the broiler for 5–10 minutes, until soft and lightly caramelized.

Serve with the crème fraîche, honey, and a scattering of pistachios.

#grilledfigs

 TART—Drizzle a little amaretto over the figs before putting under the broiler.

TWEAK—You could swap the figs for peaches: just broil for an extra 5 minutes.

TOMORROW—Any leftovers are perfect for breakfast.

Rhubarb and preserved ginger fool

Preserved ginger is gingerroot that has been preserved in sugar syrup. It's sticky and sweet. You can also get it crystallized with a sugary coating—a sort of upmarket version of a fruit pastille. Dipped in melted chocolate and left to set, it makes a good after-dinner treat.

Serves 2

7 ounces rhubarb, cut into
  1-inch chunks
¼ cup water
2 tablespoons granulated sugar
juice of ½ a lemon
2 pieces of preserved ginger,
  roughly chopped
1 heaping cup plain yogurt
a small handful of toasted sliced
  almonds (optional)

Put the rhubarb in a saucepan with the water, sugar, and lemon juice. Bring to a boil, cover, and cook over low heat until the rhubarb has softened—about 10 minutes.

Taste and adjust for sweetness—you may need to add some more sugar. Put into a mixing bowl, cover with cling wrap, and chill in the refrigerator for half an hour.

Add the chopped preserved ginger and yogurt to the chilled rhubarb and stir to combine. Serve sprinkled with sliced almonds, if you like.

#rhubarbfool

Tart—Add a drop of Cointreau to the fool.

Tweak—Instead of preserved ginger, add broken up bits of ginger snaps to the fool. If feeling indulgent you could swap the yogurt with cream. Whip ½ cup cream to soft peaks before folding in the rhubarb.

Tomorrow—This keeps well for a couple of days, so makes for an ideal desk-lunch dessert.

5-minute sponge

My sister found a cookbook from 1944 in a thrift store in Edinburgh. It's a beautiful discovery—as good a reflection of wartime baking as any. Recipes include "Economy Cake," and "Butterscotch Tart." An ambitious "Roast Duck" has been crossed out in favor of "Potato Soup."

This recipe comes from the book, although I've tweaked it a little. The sponge originally used dried egg, but I've splurged and used fresh ones. It also suggests that sponge should be baked in "a quiet oven," which is a lovely but useless instruction. I also assume the title refers to prep time, as opposed to baking time, as this actually takes more like 15 minutes to cook.

Serves 2

4 tablespoons self-rising flour
4 tablespoons superfine sugar
2 teaspoons baking powder
zest of 1 lemon
1 egg, lightly beaten
¼ cup milk
butter, for greasing
4 tablespoons light cream
a handful of berries (optional)

Preheat the oven to 325°F.

Mix the flour, sugar, baking powder, and zest together thoroughly in a mixing bowl, then whisk in the egg. Slowly add the milk and whisk until the mixture is smooth, then pour into individual greased ramekins. Place the ramekins on a cookie sheet and bake in the oven for 15 minutes. Remove and rest for 5 minutes before serving with cream. If you wanted to fancy it up a bit you could turn them out onto a plate and add a few berries.

#5minutesponge

TART—Try putting a generous blob of lemon curd in the bottom of each ramekin, or stirring some blueberries through the sponge batter.

TWEAK—Use orange zest instead of lemon zest.

3 quick ice-cream toppings

Having a good ice-cream sauce or three up your sleeve is a handy trick. The following recipes each provide a slightly quirky but excellent adornment to one of my favorite treats.

Cardamom, rum, and banana

1½ tablespoons butter
1 banana, peeled and sliced
2 tablespoons superfine sugar
10 cardamom pods
a splash of rum

This one works particularly well with chocolate ice cream —obviously chocolate and banana pair well, and chocolate and cardamom are fantastic together.

Melt the butter over medium heat and, when it's foaming, add the banana and sugar. Swill around to coat the banana and let color gently for 5 minutes, shaking the pan every now and then.
  Deseed the cardamom pods and lightly crush the seeds in a mortar and pestle. Add to the banana along with the rum and simmer for a minute or two until sticky and bubbling. Serve hot.

Va va voyages

Mom's chocolate sauce recipe

1 tablespoon butter
2 cups brown sugar
1 heaping cup heavy cream
6 tablespoons unsweetened
  cocoa powder
2 tablespoons light corn syrup
½ teaspoon vanilla extract

My sister and I weren't the most straightforward children. Most nights we'd insist Mom not bother to make dessert, only to decide that, actually, we did want something sweet. Thankfully, this recipe for chocolate sauce always meant ice cream was an appealing solution. It's good freshly made and meltingly hot, but it also keeps well in a jar in the refrigerator, perfect for last-minute changes of heart or late-night foraging. Just reheat gently.

Melt the butter in a saucepan over medium heat and add the sugar. Stir to dissolve, then simmer for a couple of minutes until fudgy. Stir in the cream, cocoa powder, corn syrup, and vanilla extract and simmer for 10 minutes, stirring occasionally, until rich and glossy. Serve hot or cold.

Pine-nut brittle

½ cup sugar
¼ cup water
4 tablespoons softened butter
a handful of pine nuts,
  roughly chopped
a pinch of salt

This caramel hardens on impact with the ice cream, creating a sticky, crunchy coating. If you prefer a fudgier caramel, whisk in a little cream along with the butter. Take care when cooking this as, when it's at its most piping, caramel is hotter than the sun.

Stir the sugar and water together in a saucepan over medium-high heat until dissolved. Bring to a boil, lower the heat, and simmer for 5–8 minutes until dark and sticky. You want to avoid stirring it at this point, but you can swill the pan round if it looks like it's at risk of burning anywhere. (Keep a close eye on it because it can turn quite quickly.)
  When the caramel is a dark whisky color, add the butter and immediately remove from the heat, whisking as you do and being careful not to splash. Add the pine nuts and salt and continue to whisk until smooth. Cool for a few minutes before serving over ice cream.

#icecreamtoppings

To wash a sticky pan, just fill it with water, bring to a boil, and simmer for a couple of minutes.

Exploring the cheap cuts

Exploring the cheap cuts

When I think of the food I love, it is rarely expensive dishes that drift into my reveries. Once in a blue moon there is something stupidly decadent and incongruous about indulging in lobster and fries, and every now and then you can't beat a fresh oyster with a glass of mouth-puckeringly dry white wine (or, even better, stout).

But I don't yearn for such things. They are a rare treat and are all the better for it. No, instead I dream of slow-roasted shoulders of lamb, cooked so tenderly that the slightest tug at a protruding shoulder blade causes the meat to fall apart and melt. I dream of roasted pork belly, the skin as crisp and brittle as a twiglet. Foie gras on toasted brioche is one thing, but give me a rustic, chunky farmhouse terrine with crusty bread any day of the week. Such food has soul.

It's these cheap cuts that require the most love and attention. While it doesn't take much intellect to make a steak taste good, these guys demand more cunning. They tend to be the parts of the animal that work the hardest, and as a result taste better but, being well-worked muscles, are also tougher. You need to care for and caress them, bathing them overnight in wine or sliding them into a low oven and leaving them to softly fall in on themselves. The fun of this cooking lies in the fact that you can plough big, gutsy flavors into a dish and then leave it to sit for, well, as long as you like, really.

More aggressive measures can work with some of these cuts, too. As with the lamb neck on p.24, you can attack the smaller tough cuts—slices of pork shoulder or skirt steak, say—with a brutal heat, the intensity of which will shock their robust fibers into submission.

With these cheap cuts, the biggest obstacle is often the shopping. They can be quite hard to find, which is why it's always worth getting to know your local butcher, if you have one. They're usually able to order in most things you might need, and of course, it's nice to support independent retailers. Otherwise there are plenty of good resources online.

Veal shank with risotto and gremolata

This is traditionally known as *ossobuco*, a northern Italian dish meaning "bone hole" because of the soft piece of marrow in the middle of the shin bone. It's this that transforms a simple, rustic dish into something spectacular. Sure, the meat is tender and delicious, but slurping down the gelatinous piece of marrow is one of the greatest pleasures in eating. Veal is no longer the pariah of the food world, just try and buy veal from ethically reared calves.

Serves 4

salt and pepper
4 x 7–9-ounce pieces of veal shank
2 tablespoons all-purpose flour
olive oil
1 onion, peeled and minced
2 stalks of celery, trimmed and minced
2 cloves of garlic, peeled and sliced
a wineglass of white wine
1¼ cups chicken stock
1 x 14-ounce can of tomatoes
a bay leaf

For the risotto
4 tablespoons butter
2 shallots or 1 small onion, peeled and minced
a stalk of celery, trimmed and minced
1⅓ cups risotto rice, Carnaroli, Arborio, or Vialone Nano
a wineglass of white wine
4 cups chicken or vegetable stock
½ cup grated Parmesan

For the *gremolata*
a handful of flat-leaf parsley
a clove of garlic, peeled and minced
zest of 1 lemon

Season the veal on both sides and coat in the flour. In a large saucepan, heat a glug of olive oil over high heat and brown the meat for a minute or two on each side. Remove to a plate, add the onion, celery, and garlic to the pan, and sweat over medium heat for 5–10 minutes, until soft. Pour in the wine, stock, and tomatoes, add the bay leaf, season with salt and pepper, and bring to a boil. Return the veal to the pan, cover, and simmer over very low heat for an hour. Remove the lid and gently simmer, uncovered, for half an hour longer to reduce.

Meanwhile, make the risotto. Put the stock in a pan and bring to a simmer. Melt half the butter in a saucepan and add the shallots or onion and celery. Season and gently cook over low heat, stirring occasionally, until soft. Increase the heat and add the rice, stirring constantly for 1 minute. Add the wine and keep stirring until absorbed. Add a ladle of stock and repeat. Continue adding a ladle of stock at a time and stirring regularly until the rice is almost cooked— about 15 minutes. Add a final ladle of stock, the rest of the butter and the Parmesan, and stir to combine.

Make the *gremolata* by mincing the parsley and mixing with the minced garlic and lemon zest. Serve the veal shank—taking care not to let the marrow slip out—with the risotto and a scattering of *gremolata*.

#ossobuco

Tart—Add a pinch of saffron to the risotto to make this into a *Risotto alla Milanese*, *ossobuco*'s traditional accompaniment.
Tweak—If you don't have the time to make a risotto, then the veal is perfectly good with boiled rice or even baby potatoes.

Braised short ribs

Tweak—As this is a basic stew recipe, you could substitute the ribs for any tough cut of beef (shin is ideal) and cook in the same way.

Tomorrow—Remove the bones and roughly chop any leftover meat. Simmer for half an hour with the stewing liquor and vegetables to make a perfect ragu for pasta.

Serves 4

1 tablespoon olive oil
2½ pounds thick short ribs, intact
salt and pepper
2 tablespoons all-purpose flour
4 tablespoons butter
1 onion, peeled and minced
2 carrots, peeled and minced
2 stalks of celery, trimmed and chopped
2 cloves of garlic, peeled and finely sliced
½ a bottle of decent red wine
1¼ cups chicken or beef stock
1 tablespoon tomato paste
a bay leaf
a pinch of sugar

"Short ribs" is, strictly speaking, the American term for these beefy behemoths. In the UK they are better known as "Jacob's ladder" but, well, I prefer calling them short ribs. It's clearer. Either way, do not equate them with their more meager piggy counterparts—there is plenty of meat on them.

Stewing and braising and the like are laughably easy, as you will see with this dish. They all require a tough or fatty cut of meat, browned for color and flavor (not to seal the meat, despite what some will tell you), vegetables, herbs, and maybe wine or beer for depth of flavor, a gentle heat, and slow cooking for softness of eating. It really is that simple, and once you've grasped this concept you can put whatever spin on it you like.

Preheat the oven to 325°F. Heat the oil in a large frying pan over high heat and, when almost smoking hot, slide in the short ribs. Season with salt and pepper and brown for a couple of minutes on each side, until well caramelized. Remove from the pan and place in a large saucepan along with the flour.

Lower the heat a little and add the butter, onion, carrots, celery, and garlic to the frying pan. Cook for 5–10 minutes, stirring regularly, until softened and caramelized, then transfer to the saucepan with the meat. Pour the red wine into the frying pan, up the heat and, while it bubbles and fizzes, scrape up any caramelized bits of meat from the pan. Add the stock and tomato paste and simmer for a couple of minutes before pouring into the saucepan. Add the bay leaf and sugar and season to taste. Cover and cook in the oven for 2 hours.

Remove from the oven and let rest for 15 minutes. Divide the ribs among four plates and serve with mashed potatoes or some soft polenta (see p.51) and a spoonful of the cooking juices.

#braisedshortribs

Rolled breast of lamb

Lamb breast is like a darker, more petite version of pork belly. It rolls easily and has the same handsome layers of fat running through it, making it an ideal candidate for stuffing and slow cooking. You'll need to start this the morning you plan on serving it, or even a day before. It really doesn't require much of your time—20 minutes at most—but, once poached, the lamb ought to cool before being sliced and fried. It's worth the wait.

Serves 4

6 anchovy fillets
a big handful of flat-leaf parsley
a small handful of mint leaves
a sprig of rosemary,
  needles picked
2 cloves of garlic, peeled
olive oil
salt and pepper
2½ pounds breast of lamb,
  off the bone
8 cups chicken stock
½ an onion, sliced
a bay leaf
a wineglass of red wine

Mince or blend together the anchovies, parsley, mint, rosemary, and garlic, and add enough olive oil to make a paste. Season with salt and pepper and spread over the inside—the nonfatty side—of the lamb. Roll it up and secure tightly with string. (Don't worry about it looking like a butcher has done it, as long as it holds you'll be fine.)

Bring the chicken stock to a boil in a large saucepan with the onion and bay leaf and lower in the lamb. Bring back to a boil, lower the heat, and gently poach for 3 hours, adding a little water or extra stock as and when needed. Turn the heat off and let cool completely in the poaching liquor.

When you're ready to serve, preheat the oven to 122°F. Remove the lamb from the poaching liquor and slice into eight slices, reserving the liquor. Heat a little oil in a frying pan over medium-high heat and fry the lamb for a couple of minutes on each side, seasoning with salt and pepper as you go. Remove to a plate and keep warm in the oven.

Pour the glass of wine into the frying pan and simmer until reduced by half, before adding a ladle of the reserved poaching liquor. Let simmer for a moment, before serving with the lamb and whatever vegetables you fancy.

#breastoflamb

TART—For a truer manifestation of a sort of inbuilt *salsa verde*, (the Italian sauce on which this stuffing is based), add capers to the herb stuffing.

TWEAK—If you can't be bothered with the rolling and chilling, gently poach the lamb unstuffed, then slice and fry before serving with the herb stuffing alongside.

Moroccan slow-roasted shoulder of lamb

Chunks of meat are all well and good, but few things beat a whole joint, slowly roasted on the bone until the meat slides away at the slightest prod. Lamb shoulder is arguably the king of such joints. It's tough as old boots but so perfectly fatty that, when sympathetically cooked, that fat melts through the meat, tenderizing and oozing flavor throughout the increasingly soft flesh.

Serves 6

1 x 3⅓–4½ pounds shoulder of lamb on the bone
1½ cups plain yogurt
juice of 1 lemon
2 tablespoons *ras-el-hanout*
½ teaspoon smoked paprika
salt and pepper
2 red onions, peeled and sliced
1 garlic bulb
½ a bottle of red wine
olive oil
1¾ cups couscous
1 pomegranate, deseeded (see opposite)
a big bunch of cilantro, chopped

Using a sharp knife, slash the lamb a few times—no deeper than an inch—on the fatty side. Mix 1 heaping cup of the yogurt, lemon juice, *ras-el-hanout*, and smoked paprika together in a bowl and season with pepper. Spread the onion out on a roasting pan, pull apart the bulb of garlic, throw in the unpeeled cloves, and place the lamb on top. Rub the lamb with the yogurt marinade, pour over the wine, cover with cling wrap, and let marinate for as long as you can—24 hours would be ideal, though an hour will do.

When ready to cook, preheat the oven to 325°F. Season the lamb with a good pinch of salt and drizzle with oil. Cover tightly with foil and roast in the oven for 3 hours. Remove the foil and roast for half an hour longer. The shoulder blade should be peeking out from under the end of the meat, if it isn't, then cook for a little longer.

Remove from the oven and let rest, loosely covered with foil, for half an hour. Meanwhile, cook the couscous according to the package instructions. Pull the meat apart with tongs, garnish with the pomegranate seeds and cilantro, and serve with a spoonful of the cooking juices, the couscous, and the remaining yogurt.

#lambshoulder

 TART—Add some wedges of eggplant to the pan before roasting.

TWEAK—For a more Italian vibe, take out the spices and yogurt and simply roast with lots of rosemary.

 TOMORROW—Any leftover lamb is fantastic in a pita with some roasted vegetables, or served with the flatbreads on p.131.

✳ To deseed a pomegranate
Cut your pomegranate in half and
put it in a bowl of water. Remove
the seeds under water; this way
they fall to the bottom while the
pith rises to the top.

Duck rillettes

Rillettes is basically a rough pâté. The meat is cooked in a low oven, basting itself in its own fat, before being pulled apart, seasoned, and set.

Serves 4 as an appetizer

salt and pepper
4 x 7-ounce duck legs
a bay leaf, torn to pieces
2 sprigs of thyme, leaves picked
7 ounces duck or goose fat
⅓ cup brandy

Sprinkle a good handful of salt over a roasting pan and lay the duck legs on top. Put another handful of salt on top, cover with cling wrap, and refrigerate overnight.

Preheat the oven to 325°F. Scrape off and discard any excess salt from the duck. Place the legs in an ovenproof dish with the bay leaf and thyme leaves. Melt the duck or goose fat with the brandy and pour over the duck. Cover with foil and cook in the oven for 2 hours.

Remove from the oven and let cool in the fat. When cool enough to handle, tug the meat from the bones with your hands, discarding the skin, bones, and any gristle. With a pair of forks, pull the meat apart until it resembles a coarse pâté. Season with pepper and add enough of the fat to coat the meat well. Pat, but don't press, into individual ramekins and cover with a little of the remaining fat. Serve at room temperature with toast and gherkins, or the pickled radishes on p.148.

#duckrillettes

Tart—You can play around with the seasonings here, adding a teaspoon of allspice at the end, or some crushed juniper berries to the melted fat.

Tweak—Follow the above recipe using chunks of pork belly instead of duck to make pork _rillettes_.

Tomorrow—Any leftover rendered duck fat will keep for months covered in the refrigerator, and is perfect for roasting potatoes in.

Chicken livers with polenta

This recipe was inspired by a chicken-liver dish I once ate at Pizza East in London's Shoreditch. I'd go back for it alone. This is my own attempt at the dish, which I think comes close to the original.

Serves 4 as an appetizer

14 ounces chicken livers
⅔ cup cornmeal
olive oil
1 shallot or small onion, peeled and minced
salt and pepper
1 small red bell pepper, deseeded and minced
1 x 14-ounce can of diced tomatoes
½ teaspoon chili flakes
a pinch of sugar (optional)
2 tablespoons flour
2 tablespoons butter
½ cup grated Parmesan
a small handful of flat-leaf parsley, minced

Wash the livers thoroughly and chop into chunks, discarding any membrane or green bile. (It won't kill you but it tastes bitter, that's all.) Let dry on paper towels.

Cook the cornmeal following the instructions opposite. Meanwhile, heat a glug of oil in a saucepan and add the shallot or onion. Season with salt and pepper, cover, and let soften over low heat—about 5 minutes. Add the pepper and sweat for another 10–15 minutes, until soft. Now add the tomatoes and chili flakes and simmer, uncovered, for 5 minutes. For a smooth sauce, blend in a blender, otherwise leave as is. Taste and add a little sugar if you feel the sauce needs to be sweeter. Keep warm over low heat.

Toss the chicken livers in the flour along with a good pinch of salt and pepper. Heat a decent glug of oil in a frying pan, add the livers, and fry for a couple of minutes on each side until crisp. Set aside on paper towels.

Add the butter and Parmesan to the polenta and stir to melt. Check for seasoning and serve with the chicken livers and tomato sauce, garnished with a little chopped parsley.

#chickenlivers

TWEAK—You could use quick-cook polenta which is done in a minute, but you have to be very much on top of things. If you don't serve it absolutely immediately then you'll end up with something akin to a rubber discus.

TOMORROW—Leftover polenta will have set. Cut it into fingers, fry in oil until crisp, and serve alongside something like a steak.

To make the polenta

Add ⅔ cup cornmeal slowly to 1¾ cups boiling water in a steady stream, whisking as you go to prevent lumps. Let cook for 40-45 minutes, stirring regularly and adding hot water as necessary, until thickened and smooth.

Lambs liver with celery root and apple mash

Lambs liver is milder in flavor than its more expensive cousin calves liver, as well as being considerably cheaper.

Serves 4

1 small celery root
salt and pepper
2 apples
4 tablespoons butter
½ teaspoon minced rosemary
1¾ pounds lambs liver,
  thinly sliced
olive oil
1 tablespoon red wine vinegar
⅓ cup red wine
⅓ cup lamb, chicken, or
  vegetable stock

Peel the celery root and cut into 2-inch chunks. Put in a pan of salted water, bring to a boil, and simmer for 10 minutes. Peel, quarter, and core the apples, add to the pan, and cook for another 10 minutes. Drain thoroughly. Return the celery root and apples to the pan over low heat and add the butter and rosemary. Season with salt and pepper and mash until smooth. Cover and keep warm.

   Season the lambs liver on both sides with salt and pepper. Get a little oil hot in a frying pan and fry the liver for 1 minute on each side. Remove to a plate to rest and add the vinegar and wine to the pan. Simmer for 1 minute before adding the stock. Simmer for another couple of minutes until reduced, and serve with the liver and mash.

#lambsliver

Tast—Garnish with "frazzled apple": Peel an apple and then, with the peeler, peel the apple flesh. Fry these peelings in hot oil until crisp and serve with the liver and mash.

Tweak—Although more expensive, calves liver works well cooked as above. In this case you could leave out the apple and add some horseradish to the mash.

Tomorrow—Use any leftover mash as the base for "bubble and squeak"; cook some cabbage and mix it through the mash before frying the whole lot until crisp and browned.

Ox cheek chili

Before you balk at the idea of cooking ox cheek and turn the page, let me just tell you—you kitchen adventurer, you—that this is hardly any different from a typical stew, Bolognese sauce, or regular chili. The same principles apply but, well, you're just using a cheek instead. It's just another muscle. So, really, there's no need for trepidation.

Serves 4

olive oil
2 x 14-ounce ox cheeks, cut into small chunks
salt and pepper
2 red onions, peeled and minced
a stalk of celery, trimmed and minced
2 cloves of garlic, peeled and sliced
2 teaspoons cumin seeds
2 teaspoons coriander seeds
2 teaspoons hot chili powder
2 cups pale ale
2 tablespoons tomato paste
1 teaspoon sugar
4 tablespoons sour cream (optional)
a handful of cilantro, minced (optional)

Heat a splash of oil over high heat in a large, heavy-bottomed saucepan and brown the ox cheeks on all sides, seasoning with salt and pepper as you go. Remove the meat and set aside. Add a little more oil to the pan, followed by the onion, celery, and garlic. Lower the heat slightly and cook the vegetables for about 5 minutes, stirring regularly, until softened and a little colored.

Crush the spices in a mortar and pestle and add to the vegetables with the chili powder. Cook for another minute or so before adding the ale. Bring to a boil and simmer for 2 minutes. Return the meat to the pan along with the tomato paste and sugar. Cover and simmer over very low heat for 3 hours. Alternatively, cook in the oven at 325°F for 3 hours.

Simmer uncovered for another 30 minutes, perhaps even an hour, until reduced and thickened. Taste for seasoning and serve however you wish—I like to garnish mine with a little sour cream and some chopped cilantro.

#oxcheekchilli

Tart—Crushed crackers are good scattered over the top of this chili. You could also add kidney beans, chickpeas, or baked beans. Just throw them in along with the tomato paste.

Tweak—If you can find them, try using chipotle chilies instead of the chili powder. They're dried and smoked jalapenos and add an incredible, fruity, smoky flavor.

Tomorrow—These sorts of dishes always taste even better a day later. Eat simply wrapped in a warm tortilla with shredded lettuce and cheese.

Two ways with skirt

You often hear of this cut of meat being referred to as *onglet*, which is the French term, or "hanger," which is the American version. Whatever you call it, it's a delicious, truly wondrous part of the cow.

Serves 4

1 x 1¾–2¼ pounds skirt steak
salt and pepper
a bay leaf
a sprig of rosemary
1 onion, sliced
2 cloves of garlic, crushed
½ a bottle of red wine
olive oil
⅓ cup chicken stock
2 tablespoons butter

Skirt steak

Place a sheet of cling wrap over the steak and bash it with a rolling pin or wine bottle until it is of a uniform thickness. Season with lots of pepper and put in a bowl. Add the bay leaf, rosemary, onion, and garlic and pour over the red wine. Cover in cling wrap and let marinate in the refrigerator for as long as you can—overnight would be ideal; a couple of hours is good, half an hour will do. Remove from the refrigerator an hour before cooking, shake off the marinade, and pat dry with paper towels. Preheat the oven to 140°F.

Put a large frying pan over high heat and add a splash of oil. When very hot, add the steak, season, and fry for 5 minutes on each side. Remove to a plate and rest in the warm oven. Tip the marinade into the pan and scrape all the caramelized bits from the bottom. Add the chicken stock and reduce by about a half. Whisk in the butter, pour in any juices from the resting plate, and keep warm. Slice the steak across the grain and serve with the gravy.

#skirtsteak

Serves 8 for nibbles or 6 as an appetizer

1 x 1 pound 2 ounces skirt steak
4 sage leaves, finely sliced
4½ ounces buffalo mozzarella, cut into small chunks
a few sprigs of rosemary (optional)
olive oil
salt and pepper
juice of ½ a lemon

Skirt and mozzarella bites

Slice the skirt steak across the grain and bash each slice with a rolling pin or other suitable implement until very thin. Cut the longer slices in half—they should be roughly 3 inches long. Finely slice the sage leaves and lay a slice or two in the middle of each strip, along with a chunk of mozzarella. Roll up each strip and skewer with rosemary sprigs or toothpicks. Drizzle with olive oil and season with salt and pepper.

Heat a frying pan over high heat with a splash of oil and add the skirt skewers. Fry for a couple of minutes, turning now and then. Remove to a plate and let rest for a minute or so. Squeeze over the lemon juice and serve.

#skirtmozzabites

Pork belly with cider and lentils

There's so much you can do with pork belly. Rubbed with five-spice, honey, and soy and left to its own devices for a few hours before roasting, it's as aromatic as a Chinese restaurant. Or, softly cooked in heart-stopping amounts of fat, it makes the most melting *rillettes*. Here it is just lightly kissed with the tang of cider and roasted simply, before being blasted at the end to crisp up the skin.

Serves 4

2½ pounds pork belly
salt and pepper
2 cups hard cider
1 onion, peeled and sliced
a bay leaf
a few sprigs of thyme,
  leaves picked

For the lentils

1 cup French green lentils,
  rinsed
olive oil
4 slices of smoked bacon,
  minced
2 tablespoons butter
1 onion, peeled and minced
a stalk of celery, trimmed and
  minced
1¾ cups chicken or
  vegetable stock
a big handful of minced flat-leaf
  parsley
a small handful of minced
  tarragon

With your sharpest knife, score the pork belly skin at ½-inch intervals and rub all over with salt. Leave for half an hour while you preheat the oven to 350°F.

Pat the pork belly dry. Pour the cider into a roasting pan and add the onion, bay leaf, and thyme leaves. Add the pork, taking care to keep the skin dry, and season with salt and pepper. Cook in the oven for an hour and a half, topping off with water if it looks as though the liquid is evaporating.

Remove the pork belly from the oven and transfer to another roasting pan. Return to the oven, turn the heat up to 425°F, and roast for another half-hour. As you finish the pork, tip the cooking juices from the first roasting pan into a saucepan and leave for 5 minutes. Skim off any excess fat from the surface and put the pan over medium heat before gently simmering to reduce.

Meanwhile, cook the lentils. Heat a little oil in a saucepan and add the bacon. Fry until crisp and remove. Add the butter, onion, and celery and sweat over low heat until soft and translucent. Add the lentils, stock, and bacon, bring to a boil, then simmer gently, covered, for 20 minutes.

When the skin has crisped up, remove the pork to a plate or carving board to rest for at least 10 minutes. Add the parsley and tarragon to the lentils and season with salt and pepper. Pull the skin off the pork and carve the meat in slices. Serve with the lentils, cider gravy, and crackling.

#porkbelly

TART—Cook a few chunks of peeled apple with the pork and mash up with a pinch of sugar for an easy apple sauce.

TWEAK—Serve the pork with roast or mashed potatoes in place of the lentils.

TOMORROW—Slice leftover pork and add to a stir-fry.

Be chatty...

We shop in a bit of a bubble at times. You don't really want to spend longer than is strictly necessary looking for your dinner, and so hanging around to chit-chat with the shopkeeper isn't always easy. It tends to annoy those standing in line behind you, too.

But being friendly makes what can be a fairly mundane operation much more fun, and you can learn a lot by talking to people. I met a crazy Polish man in a store once who told me about a soup of canned sorrel with a boiled egg, which turned out to be delicious. He also discussed a "flour and water bake" at great length, and I'm only half-sure he was joking.

In butchers' shops it's particularly useful to establish a dialogue. I worked in one for a while, and it was heartening to see how the butchers Darragh and Les had such a rapport with their customers—they knew their names and what they liked, and reveled in giving guidance to those unsure of what to do with their purchases. More often than not there was some juicy local gossip to chew over, too.

And you've got to wonder about those people you see scowling in the line at the checkout. Just how much do you think they are really going to enjoy their supper?

Pork shoulder steaks

As an entire beast the pork shoulder is quite something. Barbecued slowly it makes the central feature of a classic American pulled-pork sandwich. Cut into steaks, as here, it responds well to hot, fast cooking, the spices and lemon juice helping to tenderize the meat before its brief cooking. If you have a barbecue, it's well worth firing it up for these.

Serves 4

4 x 5-ounce pork shoulder
  steaks
2 teaspoons fennel seeds
1 teaspoon chili flakes
juice of ½ a lemon
a handful of flat-leaf parsley,
  minced
2 tablespoons olive oil
salt and pepper

Take a rolling pin and give the steaks an enthusiastic bash until they are a vaguely uniform thickness—about a thumb's width.

Crush the fennel seeds in a mortar and pestle and combine with the chili flakes, lemon juice, parsley, and olive oil. Rub all over the pork, cover, and leave for an hour.

Get a frying pan or barbecue hot. Season the steaks with salt and pepper and cook for 5 minutes on each side. Remove to a plate and rest for a couple of minutes before serving with whatever vegetables you fancy.

#porkshouldersteak

TWEAK—For an Asian twist, substitute the fennel seeds for a couple of teaspoons of Chinese five-spice and add a tablespoon of soy sauce and a little runny honey to the marinade.

TOMORROW—Leftover steak can be sliced thinly and tossed through a salad, or added to a stir-fry at the last minute.

Corner shop capers

Corner shop capers

There's a store near where I live in North London that seems to be open all night. On more than one occasion I've been coming home late and, ducking in to find some sustenance, have found my sister—who is also my roommate—doing the same thing. Sometimes the spoils are as simple as a box of cereal and a bottle of milk; at others it might be a little more complicated—pita breads to be stuffed with canned eggplant, yogurt, and spices, or peaches to be eaten standing up, straight out of the can. Such tummy-fillers are rarely ambitious or time-consuming, but they are always more satisfying, cheaper, and healthier than a burger or a bag of fries.

Not that I'm fussy when it comes to midnight munchies. I enjoy the occasional burger as much as the next man. But it's not the only option. Those late-night stores that glint with cans and cheap beer can be a surprising treasure trove of ingredients—if you know what to look for.

Food, after all, is about context. There are few recipes in this chapter that I'd recommend you serve to guests (although the Soviet salmon soup would make a quirky appetizer). These, on the whole, are recipes for you to fill your belly when other options are thin on the ground. They're for those nights when a drink after work turned into four or five and you missed supper, or when the grocery store closes on a Sunday night before you've managed to get your act together—the times when the takeout menu is at its most alluring. Here instead is a collection of dishes that can be thrown together in minutes and eaten from the saucepan standing, or curled up in front of the TV.

Persian eggplant stew with jeweled rice

Canned eggplants are a surprisingly brilliant resource. Slippery and soft, they can add great depth and texture to a dish in seconds.

Serves 2

olive oil
1 onion, peeled and chopped
salt and pepper
1 large potato, chopped
1 teaspoon turmeric
1 x 14-ounce can of eggplant, or 1 large eggplant sliced into thick circles
1 tablespoon tomato paste
zest of ½ a lemon
a small handful of cilantro

For the jeweled rice
¾ cup rice
1¼ cups water
a handful of raisins or dried cranberries
a handful of chopped pistachios

In a large frying pan or wok, heat a little oil over medium heat and add the onion. Season with salt and pepper and fry, stirring occasionally, for a few minutes, until softened and gently browned at the edges. Add the potato and fry for another 5 minutes, shaking now and then, until it starts to color. Add the turmeric, eggplant, tomato paste, and lemon zest and stir thoroughly. Add a little water—just enough to stop the bottom burning—cover, and let simmer gently.

To make the jeweled rice, put the rice and water in a medium saucepan over high heat, add a pinch of salt, and stir to break up the grains. As soon as it starts to boil, cover, and turn the heat right down. Cook for 12 minutes, then turn the heat off and leave for another 5 minutes with the lid still on. Resist any temptation to remove the lid.

Meanwhile, pour a little boiling water over the raisins or cranberries and leave for 10 minutes to swell. Drain the berries and stir through the cooked rice along with the pistachios. Serve with the eggplant stew and garnish with chopped cilantro.

#persianstew

TART—Brown a few chunks of lamb leg at the beginning and gently stew with the eggplant. This will need longer cooking—an hour should do it.

TWEAK—This dish is traditionally made using dried limes, which you can find in Middle Eastern stores. Prick a couple of limes a few times with a fork and add them to the stew along with the eggplant in place of the lemon zest.

Spinach and chickpea curry

Strictly speaking, curry from a can might not sound the most appealing dinner prospect, but that is basically what this is. And although it may appear unrefined, it is oddly satisfying—a dish that is very much more than the sum of its parts.

Serves 4

olive oil
1 red onion, peeled and minced
a clove of garlic, peeled and sliced
1 tablespoon curry powder
salt and pepper
1 x 14-ounce can of chickpeas, drained and rinsed
1 x 13-ounce can of spinach
scant 1 cup coconut milk
1 tablespoon tomato paste
juice of ½ a lemon
4 chappatis, naan, or pita

Preheat the oven to 350°F.

Heat a little oil in a medium saucepan or wok over medium heat. Add the onion and fry, stirring regularly, until soft—about 5 minutes. Add the garlic and curry powder, season with salt and pepper to taste, and stir for 30 seconds or so before adding the chickpeas, spinach, coconut milk, and tomato paste. Bring to a boil and simmer for 5–10 minutes.

Meanwhile, warm the bread in the oven. Add the lemon juice to the curry and taste for seasoning, before serving with the flatbreads.

#veggiecurry

Tart—All sorts of tarting to be done here. You could add chunks of chicken along with the curry powder and garlic, or some chopped fresh red chilies for a spicier curry. The chicken should take 8–10 minutes to cook.

Tweak—If you can find *injera*—an East African pancake-y flatbread—it's fantastic here. Its tanginess provides the perfect foil for the creamy curry.

Tomorrow—This curry will keep for a couple of days in the refrigerator.

A bean stew in seconds

Canned beans are a great source of sustenance when the refrigerator is bare. Most kinds will work for this dish, but I favor chunky lima beans. Serve with warm "French" bread—you know, the stuff you get in packages at the market—or, if you have more time, a baked potato.

Serves 2

1½ tablespoons butter
1 onion, peeled and chopped
salt and pepper
2 cloves of garlic, peeled
  and sliced
a pinch of hot chili powder
1 x 14-ounce can of lima
  beans, drained
1 x 7-ounce can of
  diced tomatoes
a splash of red wine
a pinch of sugar
a handful of flat-leaf parsley or
  basil, or both
1 ounce Parmesan cheese

Melt the butter in a medium saucepan and add the onion. Season with salt and pepper, cover, and sweat for 5 minutes, stirring occasionally. Add the garlic and chili powder and fry gently for another minute or so before adding the beans, tomatoes, red wine, and sugar. Bring to a boil and simmer for 10 minutes.

Roughly chop the parsley, or tear the basil, and stir into the stew. Check for seasoning, grate over the Parmesan, and serve.

#beanstew

TART—Brown some small Italian sausages in a frying pan and add to the stew with the beans. Or try adding some chopped kale along with the beans.

TWEAK—Substitute the chili powder for hot smoked paprika.

Smoked sausage with apples and cream

My friend Ed has the greatest propensity for dairy produce I have ever seen in a human being. For him a piece of bread is a vehicle for butter, a means of getting it to his mouth, as opposed to anything that might be delicious in its own right. He once tipped a pot of cream over a tagine I'd made, to my utter horror, and he is the only man I can imagine coming up with a dessert called *"crème à la crème"* —a dish made up of equal parts cream, raspberries, and sugar. It's fitting, then, that this, the first thing he ever cooked for me, involved cream. And very good it was, too.

Serves 2

olive oil
1 onion, peeled and chopped
1 apple, peeled, cored, and
  sliced
salt and pepper
7 ounces smoked sausage,
  kielbasa, *kabanossi*, or similar
⅓ cup heavy cream
1 tablespoon Dijon mustard
a little flat-leaf parsley
  for serving (optional)

Heat a little oil (only a little though, as smoked sausage tends to be quite greasy) in a saucepan over medium heat and add the onion and apple. Season with salt and pepper, turn the heat down, cover, and cook for 8–10 minutes, until the apples have softened but retain a little bite.

Roughly cut up the sausage and add it to the pan along with the cream and mustard. Bring to a boil, lower the heat, and simmer uncovered, stirring, for a couple of minutes until the cream has thickened. (As the sausage is already cooked you're only warming it through.) Serve scattered with chopped parsley, if you have some at hand.

#smokedsausage

TART—Stir-fry some cabbage before adding the cream and sausage.

TWEAK—If in need of a carbohydrate hit this is good stuffed into pitas or, if feeling particularly hunger-stricken, tossed through pasta.

Soviet salmon soup

This probably sounds disgusting. Canned salmon certainly isn't the most appealing ingredient, at least to any cook outside of a war zone. And a dish with the word "Soviet" in the title is unlikely to entice. But a bizarre transformation happens when you cook this dish, and something you expected to be like cat food in broth somehow tastes delicious.

Serves 2

olive oil
1 onion, peeled and chopped
a clove of garlic, peeled
 and sliced
a stalk of celery, trimmed
 and minced
salt and pepper
1 potato, chopped
 into small dice
1 teaspoon vegetable bouillon
 powder
2 cups boiling water
1 x 14-ounce can of salmon
1 teaspoon dill, fresh or dried

Heat a little oil in a saucepan over gentle heat and add the onion, garlic, and celery. Season with a little salt and pepper, cover, and sweat for 5 minutes, until soft. Add the potato and bouillon powder to the pan and pour in the water. Add the canned salmon, along with the juices from the can, and simmer for 8–10 minutes, breaking up the salmon with a wooden spoon, until the potato is cooked.
 Stir in the fresh or dried dill and serve.

#russiansoup

Tart—Add some roughly chopped kale or spinach to the soup along with the salmon. My friend Sergei also recommends adding a blob of mayonnaise on top of each portion of soup, which has a tendency to split it, but does add richness.

Tweak—To further "Russify" this dish you could substitute—or indeed augment—the potato with cooked beets for a pink, but earthy, soup.

Cheese on toast with a twist

It is often said that classics shouldn't be messed around with. In theory it makes sense; dishes are classic and simple for a reason. But how boring would life be if we just stuck to the familiar and the reliable? I'm not proposing that this is a better way to do cheese on toast, or that this is how you should do it from now on, but it wouldn't be much of a recipe if I said "make toast, slap on cheese, throw under the broiler" now, would it? All I'm saying is that a little adaptation now and then is a good thing.

Serves 2

2 tablespoons butter
1 onion, peeled and thinly sliced
salt and pepper
⅓ cup beer, plus extra
  for drizzling
2 slices of bread
½ a clove of garlic
1 tablespoon Dijon mustard
6 anchovy fillets
7 ounces cheddar cheese, sliced

Preheat the oven to 425°F.

Melt the butter in a saucepan over medium heat and add the onion. Season with salt and pepper and stir regularly until softened and slightly caramelized: around 7 minutes. Add the beer, turn the heat up a little, and simmer for 3–5 minutes, until almost entirely evaporated.

Meanwhile, rub the bread with the garlic and put on the middle shelf of the oven for 3 minutes, until lightly toasted. Remove, spread it with the mustard, and top with the cooked onion and anchovies. Lay the cheese slices on top and drizzle over a little more beer. Lay on a foil-lined cookie sheet and return to the oven for another 5 minutes, until oozing and browned. Serve not quite immediately (unless you enjoy cauterizing the roof of your mouth).

#cheeseontoast

Tart—A fried egg on top makes for a quite magnificent tart.
Tweak—For a Gallic vibe, replace the beer with white wine and the anchovies with slices of ham.

Recipes: a guide, not a gospel

Flexibility is essential when it comes to cooking. If you slavishly follow a recipe then it is easy to be flummoxed when you find that you're missing something.

Ingredients

Not all ingredients are essential to a recipe. If you follow your instincts then you should be able to work out which category an ingredient falls into. For example, in the beet soup (p.99): beets, essential; stalk of celery, less essential. Things can be tweaked and adapted. Herbs added to stews add depth but can be forgone. Whole spices can usually be swapped for ground —the flavor isn't as good, but you get the idea.

With cheese, think about what it contributes. Parmesan, say, adds saltiness and tang, so use another cheese which does this if you don't have Parmesan. Pecorino would be a good replacement, and even a really sharp cheddar will work in some dishes.

Fish is another ingredient that poses problems, as you can't always find what you're after. If it's a white meaty fish like cod that you're looking for, this can always be swapped for haddock, pollock, or monkfish. Ask the person at the fish counter if you're stuck. Don't just write off a recipe because you can't find your first-choice ingredients.

Gear

On occasion a recipe will require a blender, or a mortar and pestle, or some other bit of gear you don't have. This is usually surmountable. A sturdy bowl and a ladle or a rolling pin make a decent enough mortar and pestle, and indeed, a bottle of wine can be used in lieu of a rolling pin (probably not for bashing spices, though). Be resourceful and improvize.

Timing

The idea that timing is this all-powerful beast in the kitchen is nonsense. There's absolutely no need, on the whole, to try and have all the components of a dish ready at the same time. Meat can rest for much longer than you think in a 140°F oven. Some things do need doing last-minute. Green vegetables will lose their luster if cooked too far ahead and left to keep warm. But on the whole it's no great disaster if things don't come together symphonically. Get your prep done properly and there should never be any cause for alarm.

Sardine sandwich with tartar sauce

It's always a shame when a great ingredient sounds gross. "Sardine" hardly has you reaching for a fork, sounding like something people used to eat when spam was the only other option. As it is, they are actually rather tasty—a fine source of protein when your choices are limited.

Serves 1

1 x 4½-ounce can of sardines, drained
salt and pepper
⅓ cup flour
2 tablespoons butter
3 teaspoons mayonnaise (homemade p.164 or decent bought mayo)
½ gherkin, chopped
1 teaspoon capers, chopped
juice of ½ a lemon
1 slice of buttered bread

Pat the sardines dry with paper towels and gently roll in seasoned flour. Melt the butter over medium heat and fry the sardines for 3 minutes on each side. Meanwhile, make your tartar sauce by mixing together the mayonnaise, gherkin, capers, and lemon juice. Season with salt and pepper. Serve the sardines on buttered bread with a few dollops of the tartar sauce. Eat. Repeat if necessary.

#sardinesarnie

 TART—If you're feeling more ambitious you could bread crumb the sardines: simply dip in beaten egg after tossing in flour, then roll in bread crumbs before frying.

A pita pizza

The production of canned fried onions is possibly not the food industry's finest hour, but they do have their place in this speedy pizza recipe. If you can't find them, just fry a little chopped onion instead.

Serves 1

1 pita bread
1 teaspoon tomato paste
1 tablespoon canned fried onions
2 tablespoons cream cheese
a pinch of dried oregano
salt and pepper

Set the broiler on high. Lightly toast the pita and spread it with the tomato paste. Mix together the canned fried onions, cream cheese, and dried oregano and season with salt and pepper. Spread this on top of the pita, drizzle with olive oil, and place under the broiler for 5 minutes, until starting to color. Serve.

#pittapizza

 TART—You could tart this up with pretty much anything that you fancy—pepperoni, red bell peppers, anchovies, chorizo, chilies—whatever you like on a pizza, really.

Canned pears with ginger chocolate sauce

In the post-apocalyptic and quite frankly miserable (but well worth a read) novel *The Road*, it is the canned pears that stand out as the great delicacy of the protagonists' supplies. While I rarely find myself in such dire straits, there is no denying that a canned pear makes for a uniquely perfect treat.

Serves 2

⅓ cup heavy cream
2 ounces semisweet chocolate
  (minimum 70% cocoa solids)
½ teaspoon ground ginger
1 teaspoon sugar
1 x 14-ounce can of pear halves,
  drained

Gently heat the heavy cream in a small pan. Bring a separate small saucepan of water to a boil, then turn the heat down to the lowest setting. Nestle a heatproof bowl over the pan of water. Break the chocolate into small pieces and add to the bowl, along with the ginger and sugar. Once fully melted, slowly pour in the heavy cream, stirring as you go, and serve over the canned pears.

#tinnedpears

Tart—Add a few chopped almonds or hazelnuts to the chocolate sauce.

Tweak—Substitute the poached pears on p.119 for the canned pears.

Rice pudding with apple and cardamom compote

Food of the gods it most certainly is not, but there is a guilty pleasure to a can of rice pudding. The homemade stuff gently warms the belly and comforts, but also takes rather a long time to make —not ideal when you're tired and hungry. This is a good compromise.

Serves 2

1 apple
¼ cup water
2 tablespoons sugar
5 cardamom pods
1 x 15-ounce can of rice
  pudding

Peel, quarter, core, and roughly chop the apple and put in a saucepan with the water, sugar, and cardamom pods. Put over medium heat, cover, and stew for 10 minutes, stirring occasionally.

Meanwhile, gently warm the rice pudding in a separate pan until the odd bubble escapes through its surface. Mash up the apples and simmer uncovered for a minute or two before serving over the rice pudding.

#ricepuddinginatin

TWEAK—Use a whole star anise in place of the cardamom pods for a different flavor.

Morning missions

Morning missions

For many people, breakfast involves at best a cup of coffee and a bowl of cereal, or at least something along those lines. When you're trying to get off to work on time, ideally squeezing in some sort of shower, ironing a shirt, and looking for your socks, feeding yourself isn't top of the agenda. The last thing you need is to be scratching around the kitchen making homemade granola and churning your own butter.

Weekends are really the time for a proper breakfast. With a pot of coffee, a carton of orange juice, and the newspapers, it's one of the best parts of the weekend. Actually it's one of the best parts of the week. To be able to sit down and idle over a meal that is usually rushed is an unbeatable joy. It's a great time to catch up with roommates and family, puttering around the kitchen at your own speed and, by degrees, pulling a meal together.

That's not to say these are exclusively weekend breakfast recipes. Make the soda bread on Sunday afternoon and you have lovely toast for a few days. The breakfast raita takes all of ten minutes to make, as does the French toast. The bloody Mary, on the other hand, is probably best left for nonwork days...

Soda bread

Bread-making is perceived as this time-consuming and highly skilled practice—the business of artisans and fanatics. But the simplest loaves can be made in minutes, the only skill required being the ability to measure ingredients and stir, as in this case. Soda bread makes the most dense and comforting toast—perfect for butter or jam. Slice the bread as thinly as you can.

Makes 1 medium loaf

scant 3 cups all-purpose flour
1 teaspoon baking soda
1 teaspoon salt
⅔ cup plain yogurt
scant 1 cup whole milk

Preheat the oven to 425°F. Sift the dry ingredients into a large bowl. Mix together the yogurt and milk until smooth. Now make a well in the center of the flour mixture and pour in most of the liquid, mixing together with your hands to form a stiff dough. You don't need to knead it—just keep mixing until it has all come together, adding a little more liquid if necessary.

Turn onto a floured cookie sheet and work into a round loaf. Cut a cross in the top with a bread knife (this will help the loaf to rise), and place in the oven. After 10 minutes turn the oven down to 400°F and bake for another 45 minutes.

Remove the loaf from the oven and give the bottom a tap. It should sound hollow. If it doesn't, return to the oven and give it another 10 minutes. Put on a cooling rack and leave until cooled completely.

#sodabread

 TART—You can tart this till you're blue in the face—woodier herbs (rosemary, thyme, sage) add earthiness, particularly if serving the bread with soup or pâté or something. For a breakfast loaf, try mixing little chunks of semisweet chocolate through the dough.

TWEAK—Substitute 1½ cups of buttermilk for the yogurt and milk. This is more traditional, I believe, but you can't always find buttermilk. You could also substitute half the white flour for whole wheat.

 TOMORROW—The bread can be eaten "fresh" for about 24 hours, but will remain good for toasting for another few days after that.

English muffins

Unlike the soda bread on the previous pages, these muffins do require kneading and time to rise—they're not a speedy breakfast solution. But there's something amazingly meditative about kneading dough and letting it rise. The muffins take just over two hours to make from start to finish, but require only 15 minutes or so of your undivided attention. As a result they are best made either for a late breakfast, or done a day ahead for Sunday morning.

Makes 8-10

1¼ cups milk
1 x ¼-ounce package of dry yeast
3½ cups all-purpose flour
1 teaspoon salt
1 teaspoon superfine sugar
softened butter, for greasing

Warm the milk very gently, remove from the heat, and add the yeast. Leave for 10 minutes. This wakes the yeast up and helps it do its thing. Put the flour, salt, and sugar in a large bowl and add the milk. Mix with your hands until the dough comes together (adding a little water if necessary), then knead on a clean work surface for 10 minutes, until smooth and elastic.

Return to the bowl, cover with a kitchen towel, and leave in a warm place for an hour until it has doubled in volume. Turn onto a lightly floured surface and gently roll out. Cut into circles—ideally with a cookie cutter as it will be neater and less likely to hinder the second rise, but the top of a mug will suffice otherwise. Cover with a kitchen towel again and leave in a warm place for another half-hour until puffed up.

Grease a frying pan with a little butter, place over medium heat, and cook for about 7 minutes a side, until golden and irresistible. Eat however you wish.

#englishmuffins

Tart—Use these muffins as the base for an Eggs Benedict (p.172).

Tweak—For whole wheat muffins, substitute whole wheat flour for half of the white flour.

Tomorrow—These muffins freeze very well and can be reheated from frozen.

Homemade baked beans

These are quick and easy to make, requiring very little of your time, but resulting in a dish of comforting simplicity.

Serves 2–4

olive oil
1 onion, peeled and minced
½ teaspoon paprika
⅔ cup tomato ketchup
1 teaspoon sugar
a few shakes of Tabasco
a few shakes of Worcestershire
   sauce
salt and pepper
1 x 14-ounce can of navy beans

Preheat the oven to 300°F. Heat a little oil in an ovenproof saucepan and gently fry the onion until soft and translucent. Add the paprika and stir briefly before adding the ketchup, sugar, Tabasco, and Worcestershire sauce. Season with salt and pepper and warm through.

Drain the beans, add to the pan, and cover. Put in the oven and let bake for 90 minutes. Serve.

#bakedbeans

> TART—Add sausage in with the beans when you bake them.
>
> TWEAK—For an extra flavor kick, substitute hot smoked paprika for the ordinary paprika.

Breakfast raita

This is a sweet take on the cooling cucumber raita, a vital condiment to any hot curry. It's a soothing and mellow dish to start the day with, sweet enough to perk you up without being as cloying as a sugary cereal. Much as I love cereal, I'd rather have a bowl of this.

Makes 7 fl oz

a handful of raisins
5 cardamom pods
scant 1 cup thick plain yogurt
2 bananas, peeled and sliced
1 tablespoon runny honey
1 tablespoon toasted sliced
   almonds (optional)

Put the raisins a bowl and cover with boiling water. Leave for 10 minutes to swell. Meanwhile, remove the seeds from the cardamom pods and pound them in a mortar and pestle. Stir the ground cardamom through the yogurt and add the banana slices and honey. Drain the swollen raisins, add to the yogurt, and mix together well. Scatter with toasted almonds, if you like, and serve.

Hangover eggs

A good breakfast is essential when feeling delicate. Eggs often hit the spot, but what I really crave at this time is chili—on a purely physical level, the punchy hit of it perks you up, clearing the nostrils and generally restoring some semblance of clarity.

Scrambled eggs with chili

Serves 4

2 tablespoons butter
2 green onions, chopped
1 teaspoon coriander seeds
1 green chili, deseeded and
  minced (see p.23)
2 tomatoes, chopped
¼ teaspoon turmeric
salt and pepper
8 eggs
a handful of cilantro leaves,
  chopped

Melt the butter in a medium saucepan, add the chopped onions, and sweat them until soft and translucent: about 5 minutes. Lightly crush the coriander seeds in a mortar and pestle and add to the pan along with the chili, tomatoes, and turmeric. Season with salt and pepper and fry for a few minutes until the tomatoes are cooked through. Beat the eggs and add to the pan. Stir regularly over medium-low heat until scrambled, then scatter with chopped cilantro and serve.

Huevos rancheros

Serves 4

1 white onion, peeled
  and chopped
1 red chili, deseeded (see p.23)
  and minced
olive oil
salt and pepper
1 x 7-ounce can of diced
  tomatoes
a pinch of sugar
4 tortilla wraps
4 eggs

For the guacamole
1 avocado
juice of ½ a lime
¼ red onion, peeled and
  minced
a handful of cilantro
  leaves, chopped

Preheat the oven to 350°F. Sweat the white onion and chili in a little oil until soft: about 5 minutes. Season with salt and pepper, add the diced tomatoes and sugar, and let simmer gently for 15 minutes. Meanwhile, make the guacamole. Mash an avocado with a fork and mix with the lime juice, red onion, and cilantro. Season with a pinch of salt.

Fold 4 tortilla wraps in foil and warm in the oven for 10 minutes. Fry four eggs in a large frying pan. Spread the warm tortillas with the guacamole, then top each with a little of the tomato sauce and, finally, a fried egg.

#hangovereggs

French toast

French toast was always my favorite breakfast as a young lad. It's good to have rediscovered it.

Preheat the oven to 140°F. Melt the butter in a frying pan over medium heat.

Beat the eggs in a mixing bowl with the milk until light and frothy. Dip the bread slices briefly in the egg mixture until well coated, add to the pan, and gently fry for 2–3 minutes on each side, until golden and crisp at the edges. (You'll need to do this in batches, so keep the cooked toast warm in your cunningly preheated oven.)

On a plate, combine the sugar with a teaspoon of ground cinnamon and turn the French toast in the mix. All that is left to do now is eat.

#eggybread

Serves 4

2 tablespoons butter
4 eggs
¼ cup milk
4 thick slices of white bread,
  cut in half diagonally
2 tablespoons sugar
1 teaspoon ground cinnamon

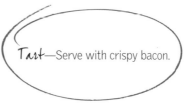

Tart—Serve with crispy bacon.

Kedgeree

If you grow your own cilantro, then try letting a plant go to seed and harvest the green coriander seeds when still young. They add an amazing citrusy edge to a dish like this. Don't worry if you don't have any however—normal coriander seeds will do just fine.

Serves 4

1 x 10-ounce fillet of undyed smoked haddock
1¾ cups whole milk
1 teaspoon crushed coriander seeds or green coriander seeds
¼ teaspoon chili powder
¼ teaspoon turmeric
1 small onion, peeled and minced
a stalk of celery, trimmed and minced
olive oil
1 cup basmati rice
salt and pepper
4 eggs
¼ cup heavy cream
2 tablespoons butter
a handful of flat-leaf parsley, roughly chopped
1 lemon, cut into wedges

Put the fish in a saucepan with the milk, coriander seeds, chili powder, and turmeric, bring to a boil, and simmer gently for 5 minutes. Remove from the heat and leave for another 5 minutes for the flavors to infuse. Carefully remove the fish, reserving the milk.

Gently fry the onion and celery in a little oil in a large saucepan until soft and translucent. Stir in the rice, season with salt and pepper, and add the reserved milk. Bring to a boil, turn the heat down to low, cover, and leave for 12 minutes. Remove the rice from the heat and leave, covered, for another 5 minutes.

Meanwhile, bring a pan of water to a boil and add the eggs, simmering for 5 minutes. Remove with a slotted spoon and put straight into a bowl of cold water. Flake the fish, discarding the skin and any bones, and peel the eggs.

Return the cooked rice to low heat and remove the lid. Add the cream, butter, parsley, and fish, and season with salt and plenty of pepper. Stir to melt the butter and serve with an egg and a wedge of lemon. You might cut the eggs in half for presentation purposes, though there's something pleasing about cutting into a perfectly runny egg.

#kedgeree

Tart—You could add a little poached salmon to this, too, or toss through some flakes of hot-smoked trout when adding the poached fish at the end.

Tweak—Use duck eggs instead of hens.

A breakfast of leftovers

It's funny how we are so mechanical when it comes to breakfast.
Were we to eat the same thing for lunch and dinner everyday we'd
get bored very quickly, yet somehow we happily munch the same
thing for breakfast, day in, day out. Perhaps it's because first thing
in the morning we're not in the frame of mind where we want to put
too much thought into what we put in our mouths. We eat largely for
sustenance, not satisfaction.

Leftovers make for a handy way of changing things up a bit.
Whether it's picking at last night's lemon tart while you wait for
the kettle to boil, or sitting down to a bowl of cold curry, there's
something fulfilling about nibbling on cling-wrapped goodies.

Mashed potato is always a happy find, making for a delicious hash,
or bubble and squeak. The recipe opposite uses mash to make potato
cakes with blood sausage and a fried egg, though this, too, can be
adapted depending on the ingredients you have to hand—it's equally
good with fish and a poached egg, for example. A cold sausage with
mustard is as delicious as any omelet in my book, while leftover pasta
carries with it the guiltiest of pleasures.

It's worth remembering the little bowl hiding at the back of your
refrigerator next time you feel like you can't face yet another bowl
of cereal.

Potato cakes with blood sausage and a fried egg

This recipe is a great way of using up leftover mashed potatoes, though it definitely merits making some up specially if you don't have any already. For this dish it doesn't matter if your mash is a little chunky and rustic, but if you favor a smooth consistency, I'd recommend investing in a potato ricer.

Serves 4

2 large potatoes
olive oil
1 small onion, peeled
  and minced
¼ cup whole milk
4 tablespoons butter
salt and pepper
1 tablespoon grain mustard
7 ounces blood sausage,
  cut into 4 circles
4 eggs

Peel and chop the potatoes, and bring to a boil in a pan of salted water. Simmer until easily skewered with a knife.

Meanwhile, heat a little oil in a frying pan over medium heat and fry the onion until soft and translucent. Drain the potatoes and leave in the colander for a minute while you gently warm the milk and butter in the same saucepan.

Return the potatoes to the pan and mash, seasoning with salt and pepper as you go. Stir in the cooked onion and mustard and let cool.

Preheat the oven to 140°F. Form the cooled mashed potato into 4 round cakes. Heat a little oil in a frying pan over medium heat, add the potato cakes, and fry for 3 minutes on each side. Remove to a plate and put in the oven to keep warm. Add the blood sausage to the pan and cook for a few minutes on each side until crisp. Place in the oven with the potatoes. Wipe the pan clean with paper towels, add the eggs, and fry. Serve the fried eggs with the potato cakes and blood sausage.

#potatocakes

TART—Dished up with a few salad greens and a sharp dressing, this makes a great appetizer.

TWEAK—A poached egg makes for a good alternative to the fried egg, while a fillet of smoked fish does likewise for the blood sausage.

Stewed fruits

Stewed fruits could just as easily have found their merry way into the preserving chapter of this book, being a wonderful means of dealing with otherwise fairly humdrum dried fruits. They keep for a good while in an airtight container in the refrigerator, and are an excellent addition to a bowl of cereal.

Makes 1 pound 13 ounces

9 ounces dried figs
9 ounces pitted dried apricots
9 ounces pitted prunes
scant 1 cup dried cranberries
1 orange, sliced
juice of 1 orange
2 tablespoons granulated or
   superfine sugar

Put the dried fruits, orange slices, orange juice, and sugar in a large saucepan and cover with water. Bring to a boil and then simmer, uncovered, for half an hour until syrupy. Let cool, cover with cling wrap, and refrigerate until needed.
   Eat these fruits on their own, with cereal, or with yogurt, oats, and all that jazz.

#stewedfruits

 Tart—Add a stick of cinnamon and a couple of whole star anise to the pan and serve the fruits with crème fraîche for a simple dessert.

Morning missions

Peanut butter and banana milkshake

It's as though the hangover never existed...

Serves 1

3 bananas
3½ cups milk
2 tablespoons chunky peanut butter
a couple of good dollops of vanilla ice cream

Put all the ingredients into a blender and blend until smooth. If you are blenderless, place all the ingredients in a bowl and mash to a pulp with a potato masher. Froth with a whisk to finish. Drink.

#pbandbmilkshake

TART—Follow my friend Dan's recommendation and add a broken-up bar of semisweet chocolate to the blender.

Chili hot chocolate

On a cold morning there are few things more enlivening than a whopping big mug of hot chocolate. While the powdered stuff does the job well enough, the homemade version is so much more indulgent and, well, chocolatey. The addition of chili adds warmth and cuts through the richness, but leave it out if it doesn't appeal.

Serves 2

4 ounces semisweet chocolate (70%), plus extra for grating
½ a dried red chili, minced, no seeds
1¾ cups whole milk
2–3 teaspoons sugar
⅓ cup heavy cream

TART—Add a splash of rum. (Probably not recommended at breakfast-time.)

TWEAK—Finish with mini marshmallows instead of whipped cream. If you don't fancy the chili, add a pinch of ground cinnamon instead.

Put a small saucepan of water on to boil, pouring the milk into a separate pan and gently warming at the same time. Sit a heatproof mixing bowl over the pan of water and break the chocolate into it. Turn the heat down and let the chocolate melt.

Once melted, add the chili and sugar and slowly pour in the warm milk, stirring as you go. Keep warm over the pan of gently simmering water while you whip the cream in a bowl until it forms soft peaks. Decant the hot chocolate into mugs, top with the whipped cream, and a little grated chocolate, if you like.

#chillihotchoc

To froth the milk

Make sure that the milk is fairly hot and whisk vigorously for a minute or two. This will force air through the milk and create the light, frothy foam you want for your latte.

Latte without a machine

A good, strong coffee with lots of frothy milk is a treat to wake up to, but it is somehow perceived as being something that requires lots of whiz-bang gadgetry and a barista diploma. Not so.

Serves 1

⅓ cup milk
coffee
unsweetened cocoa powder or finely grated chocolate, for sprinkling

Pour the milk into a medium saucepan and warm gently over medium heat, taking care not to boil.

Meanwhile, make a small pot of strong coffee. While the coffee is brewing, check that the milk is steaming (it needs to be fairly hot in order to whisk properly) and whisk vigorously for a minute or two. Half-fill a large mug with coffee and top off with the frothy milk. Sprinkle with cocoa powder or finely grated chocolate if you like.

#latte

Bloody Mary

The addition of grapefruit juice here adds an extra balance of sweet and sharp. You don't have to mix this in a mixing glass first, but, unless stirred well, the horseradish tends to sit in little clumps. It also means the vodka is mixed well throughout the drink, as opposed to sitting like a boozy little surprise at the bottom of your glass.

Serves 1

¼ cup vodka
¼ cup grapefruit juice
⅔ cup tomato juice
1 teaspoon grated horseradish
a few shakes of Tabasco
a few shakes of Worcestershire sauce
pepper
a pinch of celery salt (optional)
a stalk of celery, trimmed
a slice of lemon

Put the vodka, grapefruit juice, tomato juice, and horseradish in a mixing glass and stir or whisk thoroughly. Add the Tabasco, Worcestershire sauce, pepper, and celery salt, if using, and mix again. Pour over ice in a tall glass, garnish with the celery stalk and lemon slice, and serve.

#bloodymary

Tweak—Replace the Tabasco and vodka with a shot of Chili Vodka (p.158), or use lemon vodka instead.

Formal forays

Formal forays

When I say "formal," I don't mean white tie and tiaras, crystal Champagne glasses, and fish knives. There's a time and a place for buttoned-up eating but I don't think the home is it. Eating at home should—in any context—be comfortable and convivial. Nothing kills conversation more than feeling that you've got to be on your best behavior.

Cooking, therefore, should be equally mellow. It's not very conducive to entertaining if you're careering back and forth from the kitchen to the dinner table, neglecting both the food and your guests in equal measure. Dishes should require the minimum of last-minute attention and effort.

But that doesn't mean the food can't be special or impressive. It's all very well trying to keep things laid-back, but if you produce a bowl of pasta for your girlfriend's birthday she might feel a little put out. With these recipes I've tried to provide dishes that look elegant and romantic, and that taste exciting and different, but that aren't going to make you sweat too much—or at least not when you've got guests who need their drinks topped off.

To make the goat curd

Line a strainer with a piece of cheesecloth or a clean dish cloth. Put it over a bowl and pour scant 2 cups of goat-milk yogurt into the cheesecloth. Add a pinch of salt, stir, cover with cling wrap, and let strain for a day or two before using.

Beet soup with goat curd

Beets and goat cheese are one of those classic food couples—they just make sense together. I often simply roast the beets in balsamic vinegar and garlic, before serving them with goat cheese and crusty bread. This is a slightly different way of combining the two. The curd is easy to make, but you do need to do it a day or two in advance. If you lack the time, then you can buy goat curd, or alternatively just use goat cheese.

Serves 6 as an appetizer

1 pound 2 ounces beets
salt and pepper
2 tablespoons butter
1 large onion, peeled
  and chopped
a stalk of celery, trimmed
  and chopped
5 cups vegetable or
  chicken stock
goat curd (see opposite)
a small handful of sliced chives

Clean the beets but don't trim the ends or peel, or you'll lose some color when you boil them. Put in a saucepan with a pinch of salt and cover with cold water. Bring to a boil and simmer until cooked— this could take 20 minutes, it could take an hour, depending on the size of the beets. When they're cooked they should be easily skewered with a knife. Drain and let cool.

Meanwhile, melt the butter in a saucepan over gentle heat. Add the onion and celery, season with salt and pepper, and sweat gently until soft and translucent.

Trim the beets and slide off the skin—it should come away when rubbed with a thumb. Roughly chop and add to the pan along with the stock. Bring to a boil and simmer for 5 minutes or so, then blend until smooth. Taste for seasoning and adjust if necessary.

Ladle the soup into bowls and serve with a dollop of goat curd and a scattering of sliced chives.

#howtrootannn

 TART—Lightly toast a handful of sesame seeds in a dry frying pan and sprinkle over the goat curd.

TWEAK—Use natural ready-boiled beets in place of raw beets to save time.

TOMORROW—Leftover soup is always a good thing to have in the refrigerator. Any leftover goat curd is amazing on toast with a little pepper and a drizzle of olive oil.

Grilled eggplant with tahini and pomegranate

I'm into vegetarian appetizers. I say that; I'm pretty much into any kind of appetizer—it's a vital course. Diving straight into the main sometimes just feels wrong, like going into the theater just as the movie starts. You need the trailers to whet your appetite.

A perky vegetarian appetizer is often just the thing —not so heavy that it ruins the rest of the meal, but enough to get you revved up for what's to come. The beauty of this one is that the eggplant can be served either hot—fresh off the grill with blistered skin and blackened flesh—or cold, when its flesh has softened and mellowed.

Serves 6 as an appetizer

juice of ½ a lemon
2 teaspoons tahini
salt and pepper
3 tablespoons olive oil
2 large eggplants,
  cut diagonally into
  ½-inch thick pieces
1 pomegranate, deseeded
  (see p.47)
2–3 handfuls of arugula

Whisk the lemon juice and tahini together with salt and pepper, then slowly pour in 2 tablespoons of olive oil, whisking as you go, until combined. Set aside.

Heat the remaining olive oil in a griddle or frying pan and fry the eggplant slices for a minute or two on both sides—seasoning with salt and pepper as you go—until nicely charred and cooked through. You'll need to do this in batches. Arrange on a large plate or six smaller ones, scatter with the pomegranate seeds and arugula leaves, and drizzle with the tahini dressing. Serve.

#grilledauberginesalad

Tart—Serve as an accompaniment to a main course with broiled lamb or chicken.

Tweak —If you're feeling lazy you can always buy ready-popped pomegranate seeds. They're often cheaper than whole pomegranates, as it happens.

Skate cheeks with pea puree and pea shoots

Among a fish's finest assets are its cheeks. From the jowly, baby's-fist-sized lumps of the monkfish to the minute, mouse's eyeball of a trout, the cheek is the most tender and flavorful of a fish's parts. You should be able to pick up some skate cheeks at your local fishmonger.

As this dish requires last-minute preparation, you're better off serving it before something you can do in advance, such as the spiced lamb (p.111) or Szechuan duck (p.109).

Serves 6 as an appetizer

a wineglass of white wine
1 bay leaf
2–3 sprigs of thyme
a small handful of parsley stalks
½ onion, peeled and sliced
a stalk of celery
salt and pepper
2⅔ cups frozen peas
2 tablespoons butter
a small handful of mint
  leaves, chopped
12–18 skate cheeks
2 ounces pea shoots
olive oil

Fill a saucepan with water along with the white wine, bay leaf, thyme, parsley stalks, onion, and celery. Bring to a boil and simmer for 10 minutes.

Meanwhile, bring a separate pan of salted water to a boil. Add the peas and simmer for 3 minutes. Drain, put in a bowl with the butter and mint, and blend or mash to a purée. Season with salt and pepper and set aside.

Drop the skate cheeks into the pan of simmering water and poach gently for 3 minutes. Remove with a slotted spoon and serve immediately with the pea purée, a few pea shoots, and a drizzle of olive oil.

#skatecheeks

⇒ TART—Fry some smoked bacon until crisp and serve scattered over the salad.

⇒ TWEAK—Try getting hold of some lovage and replace the mint with a few of its aromatic leaves. Fava beans would also make a good substitute for peas—if you have the patience to pod them, that is.

Beef carpaccio with horseradish remoulade

The story goes that in 1950 an Italian countess, who I imagine must have been fat as a barrel, waddled into Harry's Bar in Venice and declared that her doctor had told her that she could only eat raw meat. The chef produced very thin slices of raw beef with a little dressing, and the dish was named after the Venetian painter Vittore Carpaccio. Serving such an Italian dish with a very French salad like *remoulade* might therefore seem perverse, but food is about flavor, not diplomacy, and beef, celery root, and horseradish are natural bedfellows.

Serves 6

10 ounces beef tenderloin steak
1 small celery root
8 tablespoons mayonnaise (homemade p.164 or decent bought mayo)
juice of 1 lemon
2 tablespoons grated horseradish
a small bunch of minced flat-leaf parsley
salt and pepper
2 tablespoons capers
olive oil

Thinly slice the tenderloin. Taking a slice at a time, lay the meat under a sheet of cling wrap, bash with a rolling pin until paper-thin, and lay on a plate. Repeat with the remaining slices, cover with cling wrap, and refrigerate until needed, removing an hour before serving.

Peel the celery root and discard the peelings. Grate into a bowl and mix with the mayonnaise, lemon juice, horseradish, and parsley. Season with salt and pepper to taste.

When ready to serve, arrange the carpaccio on one large or six separate plates. Pile the *remoulade* over the center of the beef slices, scatter over the capers, and drizzle with olive oil. Serve.

#carpaccio

Tart—Mince some hazelnuts and scatter with the capers.

Tweak—Swap the horseradish for grainy mustard in the celery root *remoulade*.

Tomorrow—Any leftover *remoulade* is delicious on toast.

Stuffed tomato

There's a good reason a stuffed tomato is a classic: it's so versatile, giving you the freedom to stuff it with pretty much whatever you fancy. As a veggie alternative at a dinner party it sits proud and handsome on the plate, and shows that you've actually put some thought into what to serve your vegetarian guests. But it would be just as happy whipped out for a picnic or served as a summer lunch in the garden.

Serves 6

1 red onion, peeled and minced
1 heaping cup couscous
1 fresh red chili, deseeded and minced
a handful of cilantro, chopped
5 ounces feta cheese, crumbled
zest and juice of ½ a lemon
2 tablespoons olive oil, plus extra for frying
salt and pepper
6 large beefsteak tomatoes

Preheat the oven to 350°F. Heat a little oil in your frying pan and fry the onion until soft. Put the couscous in a bowl and pour over enough boiling water just to cover it. Cover with a kitchen towel and leave for 5 minutes. Fluff with a fork and stir in the onions, chili, cilantro, feta, lemon zest and juice, and olive oil. Season to taste and set aside.

Cut the tops off the tomatoes but don't throw them away. Scoop out the insides with a spoon and discard. (If you feel guilty about the waste, you can always make some salsa out of this flesh, see p.126 for my recipe for Tomato and Avocado Salsa).

Season the cavity and cram the couscous combo into each tomato, before then plonking the lids back on top. Drizzle with olive oil and roast in the oven for half an hour. Serve hot or cold.

#stuffedtomato

TART—Add chunks of roasted butternut squash to the couscous.

TWEAK—Replace the lemon zest and juice with a chopped preserved lemon.

Broiled sea bream with tomato salad

You don't always necessarily want a heavy main course. If you're giving your guests something to nibble on with drinks—whether it's potato chips or elaborately constructed canapés—and then an appetizer, a big old entree is often overkill. Something light and delicate like this is often more appropriate, and leaves room for copious amounts of cheese afterward. If, however, you find that you do want to bulk this up, then serve with potatoes, green salad, or whatever else you fancy. After all, it's your dinner.

Serves 6

6 x 5-ounce fillets of sea
  bream, scaled
a few sprigs of thyme
  or oregano
olive oil
juice of ½ a lemon
2 tablespoons capers

For the tomato salad

1 pound 2 ounces of the best
  tomatoes you can find, at
  room temperature
a pinch of granulated sugar
salt and pepper
1 shallot, peeled and
  finely sliced
a handful of basil leaves, torn

Preheat the broiler to its highest setting.

Make the tomato salad by slicing the tomatoes or roughly chopping into chunks. Put in a bowl with the sugar and season generously with salt and pepper. Add the sliced shallot, basil leaves, and a good glug of oil and stir well. Taste for seasoning and set aside.

With a sharp knife, score the bream's skin at ½-inch intervals. (You don't have to be too finicky about this, but it helps the skin to crisp up and stops it from curling up under the heat.) Tuck the thyme or oregano sprigs into the slits, drizzle with olive oil, and season on both sides with salt and pepper. Put under the broiler, skin-side up, for 5 minutes, then remove and rest for a minute. Serve with the tomato salad, squeezing with the lemon juice and scattering with the capers.

#seabream

Tart—Add a little chopped red chili to the tomato salad for a piquant edge.

Tweak—While broiling fish avoids stinking up the kitchen when you've got guests, if you'd prefer to fry in oil, then fry for 3 minutes on the skin-side before turning and frying for another minute. Serve.

Tomorrow—Make bruschetta by mashing leftover tomato salad and spreading onto toasted sourdough.

Roasted cod with a warm Russian salad and aïoli

TART—Wrap the cod in slices of Serrano ham. For that authentic Russian experience, serve with chilled vodka.

TWEAK—Use yogurt instead of mayonnaise in the aïoli.

TOMORROW—The salad works well for lunch, particularly with some smoked mackerel added.

Serves 6

1 pound 2 ounces beets
salt and pepper
6 x 5–7-ounce skinless fillets of
  sustainably sourced cod
3 tablespoons olive oil
4 green onions, trimmed and
  finely sliced
2 tablespoons minced gherkins
1 tablespoon Dijon mustard
2 teaspoons white-wine vinegar
a small handful of dill,
  minced
a small handful of flat-leaf
  parsley, minced
2 tablespoons olive oil
juice of ½ a lemon

For the aïoli
3 tablespoons mayonnaise
  (homemade p.164 or decent
  bought mayo)
a clove of garlic, peeled and
  crushed to a paste
  (see opposite)

In 1952, a book was published in Soviet Russia called *The Book of Healthy and Tasty Food*. For about 30 years it was one of the most widely used Russian cookbooks, but was far from easily available. In fact, it was so valuable that it became a form of currency, and families lucky enough to have a copy would use it as a bargaining tool with a busy doctor or the police. It's a fascinating piece—thousands of pages of propaganda filled with great spreads of meats and wines served on ornate plates in opulent dining rooms. The recipes themselves don't quite reflect such decadence, but many of them are nevertheless delicious, such as this one for vinaigrette—not a dressing, as you might think, but a warm salad.

Preheat the oven to 400°F. Wash the beets and boil in a pan of salted water until easily pierced with a skewer. This could take anything from 20 minutes to an hour, depending on the size of the beets. When the beets are cooked, drain and set aside.

Place the cod in a roasting pan, season with salt and pepper, drizzle with a tablespoon of olive oil, and roast in the oven for 10–12 minutes, until cooked (it should be firm to the prod and of a uniform whiteness).

Meanwhile, trim the beets and slide off the skin with your thumb—it should come away easily. Dice into small cubes and toss with the green onion, gherkins, mustard, vinegar, dill, parsley, and the remaining olive oil. Season with salt and pepper.

For the aïoli, place the mayonnaise and garlic in a bowl and stir to combine. Arrange the roasted cod and warm salad on plates, squeeze with the lemon juice, and serve with the aïoli.

#warmrussiansalad

To crush a clove of garlic
Flatten it with the side of a large knife and remove the peel. Add a pinch of salt to the garlic and crush to a paste with the knife.

Formal forays

Pea pilaf with spiced crispy shallots and almonds

This is the sort of dish that I would happily go vegetarian for—fragrant and soft, it all at once enlivens and soothes. Serve as an entree or, if you can't cope without meat, alongside a goat curry (see p.134).

Serves 6

olive oil
1 onion, peeled and minced
2 stalks of celery, trimmed and minced
2 cloves of garlic, peeled and sliced
salt and pepper
2 teaspoons ground coriander
1 whole star anise
a stick of cinnamon
1 clove
1½ cups basmati rice
2½ cups vegetable stock
1¾ cups frozen peas
½ cup sliced almonds
3 shallots, peeled and finely sliced
½ teaspoon hot chili powder
a good handful of cilantro leaves

Heat a little oil in a large saucepan over medium-low heat and add the onion, celery, and garlic. Season with salt and pepper, cover, and sweat for 10 minutes. Add the coriander, star anise, cinnamon stick, and clove and stir for a minute or two before adding the basmati rice. Stir thoroughly to coat the rice grains with the oil and spices, then add the stock, prodding a little with a spoon to break up the grains. Bring to a boil, turn the heat down to low, cover, and cook for 15 minutes. Resist the urge to remove the lid—you need to keep the steam in there.

Meanwhile, bring a pan of salted water to a boil. Add the peas and cook gently for 2 minutes. Drain and run under cold water for 30 seconds.

Take the rice off the heat and leave, covered, for 5 minutes. Heat a dry frying pan over medium heat and add the almonds. Keep tossing until lightly toasted here and there (being careful not to burn) and tip into a bowl. Put the pan back on high heat and add about ¼ inch of oil. When the oil is good and hot, add the shallots and fry for 30 seconds to a minute, until crisp. With a slotted spoon, remove to a bowl lined with paper towels, sprinkle with chili powder, and season with salt.

Uncover the rice and let it sit for a couple of minutes, before fluffing with a fork and stirring in the peas. Taste for seasoning and garnish with the crispy shallots, toasted almonds, and cilantro. Serve.

#peapilaf

TART—Try adding chunks of paneer to the pilaf to give it a protein and texture boost.

TWEAK—Substitute fava beans for the peas.

 TOMORROW—Leftover rice gets bad press, but I've been eating it all my life and it's never done me any harm. Just make sure you put it in the refrigerator as soon as possible.

Szechuan duck

Szechuan pepper is an amazing seasoning. Its evocative aroma—ancient and fiery—seems to have millennia of Chinese history imbued in its heady notes. The amount used in this recipe might seem like a lot, but the point of this dish is that it is nostril-clearing and punchy. Serve it with gently seasoned Chinese cabbage or bok choy and some sticky rice, which should offset the duck perfectly.

Serves 6

2 tablespoons Szechuan
  peppercorns
2 tablespoons soy sauce
1 tablespoon sunflower oil
1 tablespoon runny honey
1 teaspoon salt
1 x 5½-pound duck

Preheat the oven to 425°F. In a dry frying pan, toast the peppercorns over medium heat (taking care not to burn) until their waft tickles your nostrils. Tip into a mortar and pestle and pound until crushed but not too powdery. Add the soy sauce, oil, honey, and salt and stir to combine.

Prick the duck all over with a fork—this helps to render the fat and crisp the skin, as well as helping the meat absorb the rub—and put it in a roasting pan. Tip over the peppercorn rub, coating the duck thoroughly, and put in the oven. Roast for 20 minutes before turning down to 300°F and roasting for another 1½ hours.

Take out of the oven and let rest for a few minutes before carving. Serve with your chosen accompaniments.

#szechuanduck

TART—Stuff a few slices of orange and gingerroot into the cavity of the duck for extra flavor.

TWEAK—Use a tablespoon of Chinese five-spice instead of Szechuan pepper.

TOMORROW—Any leftover duck can be made into pancakes with plum sauce and shredded lettuce. And pancakes, obviously.

Formal forays

Rabbit with mustard and cream

There are some nights when a belly-coddlingly, breast-beatingly rich stew just hits the spot. When frost kisses the windowpanes and your breath hangs on the air, this is the time to stuff yourself to the gullet with robust food. Nowadays you can find rabbit in specialty markets, but failing that give your butcher a day or two's notice and he'll get you some in.

Serves 6

olive oil
2 strips of smoked bacon,
  roughly chopped
2 rabbits, jointed
salt and pepper
2 tablespoons all-purpose flour
2 tablespoons butter
2 onions, peeled and sliced
a stalk of celery, minced
a clove of garlic, peeled
  and sliced
2 cups hard cider
1¼ cups chicken stock
a sprig of thyme
1 bay leaf
scant 1 cup heavy cream
3 tablespoons Dijon mustard
a handful of flat-leaf parsley

Preheat the oven to 350°F.

Heat a drop of oil in a large saucepan over medium heat, add the bacon, and fry until crisp. Remove with a slotted spoon and set aside.

In your biggest mixing bowl, season the rabbit with salt and pepper and add the flour. Coat the rabbit pieces in the flour and brown in the bacon fat over medium-high heat until colored on all sides. You'll need to do this in batches, adding a little more oil as necessary. Remove from the pan. Add the butter, onion, celery, and garlic and cook for a few minutes, stirring constantly, then pour in the cider and chicken stock. Bring to a boil and add the rabbit, bacon, thyme, and bay leaf. Cover and cook in the oven for around 1½ hours.

Remove from the oven, uncover, and place over medium heat. Stir in the cream and mustard and simmer gently, uncovered, for another 15 minutes (if you need more time to do your vegetables, then you can always leave it for longer). Roughly chop the parsley and stir through the dish. Taste for seasoning and serve with whatever vegetables you fancy.

#mustardrabbit

TART—For a really indulgent stew, swap the bacon for big, rustic chunks of pork belly or hunks of chorizo. Or both.

TWEAK—If you'd prefer a healthier version of the stew, then simply omit the cream.

Spice-roasted leg of lamb with cumin potatoes

A leg of lamb is one of the most handsome and generous things you can cook for your friends. Simply roasted with lots of rosemary and garlic there is an understated beauty to it, compared with something more Neanderthal like a rib of beef. It's probably my favorite Sunday lunch: familiar and comforting. But marinated in spices and almonds and roasted to a soft, medium pinkness, it is utterly stupendous—as aromatic as a Mumbai breeze and spicier than a D. H. Lawrence novel.

Serves 8-10

a bunch of cilantro
2 teaspoons ground coriander
2 shallots, peeled and chopped
4 cloves of garlic, peeled
 and sliced
4 fresh Thai chilies, stalks
 removed
2 tablespoons plain yogurt
4 tablespoons ground almonds
juice of 1 lemon
olive oil
1 x 5½-pound leg of lamb
salt and pepper
3⅓ pounds baby potatoes
1 tablespoon cumin seeds

Tart—Not much tarting required, in my opinion.

Tweak—Use goat meat instead of lamb.

Tomorrow—Any leftover lamb is amazing wrapped in naan with lots of shredded vegetables and yogurt.

If you have one, put the fresh cilantro and ground coriander, shallots, garlic, chilies, yogurt, almonds, and lemon juice in a blender and blend to a smooth paste, pouring in a little oil as you go until spreadable in consistency. If blenderless, you'll need to chop the cilantro, shallots, garlic, and chilies separately as fine as you possibly can and mix with the ground coriander, yogurt, almonds, and lemon juice in a bowl, loosening up with a little oil.

Slash the lamb a few times on the skin-side with a sharp knife, and rub all over with the paste. Let marinate for at least a couple of hours, ideally overnight. Just make sure you take the lamb out of the refrigerator at least 1 hour before cooking.

Preheat the oven to 375°F. Season the lamb with salt and pepper, drizzle with olive oil, and roast for 1½ hours. About 1 hour into cooking, cut the potatoes into equal size chunks and bring to a boil in a pan of salted water. Remove the lamb from the oven and rest, loosely covered in foil.

Meanwhile, put a frying pan over medium heat and add the cumin seeds. Shake around a little and, once you can smell the aroma of the spice, remove from the heat and lightly crush in a mortar and pestle. When the potatoes are cooked, drain and toss in the crushed cumin, seasoning with salt and pepper.

Carve the lamb and serve with the potatoes and some mango chutney or raita (yogurt, chopped cucumber, and mint), or perhaps the cilantro salad on p.133.

#spicedlamb

Pork Wellington

A traditional beef Wellington is something to behold, but that much beef fillet costs a fortune. Pork tenderloin works as a more affordable alternative, sitting nicely alongside the mushrooms and the mustard. It's also lean enough not to fill you up completely, as is often the case with pork.

Serves 6

4 strips of unsmoked bacon, finely sliced
olive oil
1 onion, peeled and chopped
salt and pepper
a clove of garlic, crushed
1 pound 2 ounces field mushrooms, sliced
⅔ cup hazelnuts, minced
a handful of flat-leaf parsley, minced
juice of ½ a lemon
1-pound 2-ounce block of ready-made puff pastry
4 tablespoons Dijon mustard
2 x 14-ounce pork tenderloins
1 egg, beaten

Heat a drop of oil in a saucepan over medium heat, add the sliced bacon, and fry until crisp. Add the onion, season with salt and pepper, and fry until the onion is soft and lightly caramelized—about 5 minutes. Now stir in the garlic and mushrooms and cook for another 5 minutes, until the mushrooms have softened. Stir in the hazelnuts, parsley, and lemon juice and let cool. You can blend the stuffing in a food processor to a smooth paste at this point if you fancy—I quite like the rustic version, but if you're going for something more refined, blend away.

Preheat the oven to 400°F. Cut the pastry in half and roll each section out until large enough to house the pork. Spread the mustard down the center of each pastry half and do the same with the stuffing. Place a pork loin on top of the mustard and stuffing in the middle of one of the pastry sheets. Brush a little beaten egg around the edges of the pastry and roll it around the pork. Trim off any excess pastry and brush all over with the beaten egg (this gives it a nice glossy finish). You could cut shapes with the trimmings to stick on—leaves and whatnot—if you feel like it. Repeat with the other loin and pastry half.

Slide the Wellingtons into the middle of the oven and bake for 20 minutes. Let rest for 10 minutes before cutting into thick portions and serving.

#porkwellington

TART—For a real treat, add some black truffle paste to the stuffing.

TWEAK—Substitute English mustard for French. If one of your guests is allergic to nuts you could happily omit the hazelnuts.

TOMORROW—Any leftover stuffing is good on toast, or warmed through with a little cream and tossed through pasta.

How to be a happy cook

There are a few things worth keeping in mind when cooking. They'll
make the process more enjoyable, tidier and, ultimately, better. Some
of them might appear a little banal but better to err on the side of
being precious than to have a kitchen that looks like a bomb site.

Before you start
Tidy the kitchen. It makes such a difference. If you start off cooking
in a mess, then God only knows what the kitchen will look like by the
end. And, call it feng shui if you like, mentally it's a lot easier to cook
in a clean and tidy kitchen.

  Read the recipe through at least once. I know this sounds boring as
hell, but it's vital. The number of times I've done all the prep without
reading the recipe, only to find I've got to let something marinate
for a couple of hours and now the potatoes are going brown and the
parsley is all floppy and oh God the dog's got at the bacon—it's worth
the effort.

  Do your mise en place. Get everything you need in order before you
start to cook. Nothing makes you sweat like having to weigh, peel,
and chop something at a crucial moment. There's more on prepping
on p.135.

When you're cooking
Keep a bowl for waste. Trying to chop an onion on a board covered
in potato peelings and onion skin is a quick way to lose a finger. It
makes cleaning up easier, too.

  Take your time. Better to have dinner 15 minutes late than to be in a
blind panic.

  Put some music on. This sounds very "self-help" but it's remarkable
how pleasant the more tedious jobs can be when there's a distraction.

  Wash up as you go. Not only does it make cooking easier, but it
means that after dinner there isn't a mountain to climb.

Cocktails

TWEAK—Make a rhubarb vodka and tonic using the rhubarb vodka on p.158.

Makes 6 drinks

1¼ cups gin
1 egg white
4 cups tonic water
2 handfuls of ice cubes

For the rhubarb syrup
10 ounces rhubarb, trimmed
4 tablespoons superfine sugar
1¼ cups water
juice of 1 lemon

Rhubarb Gin & Tonic

A pink twist on a classic, the egg white gives this cocktail its foamy head. If you don't have a cocktail shaker then whisk together in a measuring cup instead.

Make the rhubarb syrup by chopping the rhubarb and throwing it in a saucepan with the sugar, water, and lemon juice. Cover and simmer over low heat for 10 minutes. Strain the liquid through a strainer and chill. Put your cocktail shaker or measuring cup, and ideally the serving glasses, in the freezer to chill.
  When ready to serve the drinks, put the gin, syrup, and egg white in the cocktail shaker and give it a good shake. (Depending on the size of your shaker you may need to do this in 2 batches.) Pour the rhubarb gin over ice and top off with tonic water.

#rhubarbgandt

Serves 1

6 mint leaves
2 teaspoons granulated sugar
1 teaspoon water
ice
scant ⅓ cup bourbon

Mint Julep

This classic from the American South isn't shy, and nor will you be after a couple. Consume in moderation, or something approaching it.

In the bottom of a tumbler, lightly bash the mint, sugar, and water and leave for a minute. Fill the glass with ice and pour in the bourbon. Stir and serve.

#mintjulep

Serves 1

ice
scant ⅓ cup good-quality vodka, from the freezer
a dash of grenadine

Sam znaesh chto

This Russian firewater, literally "you know what" in English, was invented and named by a friend in a Moscow bar in answer to the constant question, "What are you drinking?" And you know what? It's pretty good.

Chill a tumbler in the freezer if you can, before filling it with ice. Pour in the vodka and add the grenadine. Stir and serve.

#youknowwhat

Formal forays

Chocolate, chili, and cardamom tart

Drop any preconceptions that I have completely lost my mind here and please have a go at this tart. It will knock your socks off, and your guests will think you're a total wizard.

Serves 8

1 x basic piecrust pastry recipe (p.178) or 10 ounces ready-made piecrust pastry
3 eggs, 1 beaten
1 heaping cup heavy cream
½ cup whole milk
2 tablespoons superfine sugar
7 ounces semisweet chocolate (minimum 70% cocoa solids)
4 ounces milk chocolate
10 cardamom pods
½ teaspoon hot chili powder
salt
scant 1 cup light cream

Lightly flour a clean work surface and roll out the pastry. Line a 10-inch tart pan with the pastry and prick all over with a fork. Chill in the refrigerator for 30 minutes (or the freezer for 10). Preheat the oven to 350°F.

Line the pastry shell with parchment paper and fill with baking beans or rice. Bake in the oven for 20 minutes. Discard the parchment paper and beans and brush the pastry all over with the beaten egg. Put back in the oven for 5 minutes until golden. Remove from the oven and turn down to 315°F.

Meanwhile, put the cream, milk, and sugar in a medium saucepan and whisk over medium heat until the sugar has dissolved. Bring to just below boiling point and remove from the heat. Break the chocolate into pieces and stir it into the hot cream, leaving to melt completely. Lightly crush the cardamom pods and remove the little black seeds. Crush these in a mortar and pestle and add to the mix along with the chili powder and a pinch of salt. Finally, beat the remaining eggs and stir into the mix until glossy. Tip this into the tart shell and bake in the oven for 20 minutes, until set.

Remove and let cool completely before serving with the light cream.

#chocolatetart

 TART—Add the zest of an orange to the chocolate. If feeling more ambitious, you could stew some cherries in Kirsch and serve them alongside. Popping candy sprinkled over the tart is quite amusing.

TWEAK—To save time you could always buy ready-made (and even ready-rolled) pastry. Avoid the ready-baked tart shells, though, which are mostly terrible.

 TOMORROW—This tart will keep happily in the refrigerator for a few days.

Formal forays

Peach zabaglione

More and more people seem to be wheat and dairy-intolerant these days, and so desserts especially can be a bit of a headache. The beauty of zabaglione, which can be served hot or cold, is that it is rich and creamy but dairy-free.

Serves 6

scant 1 cup Marsala
8 tablespoons sugar
3 underripe peaches, peeled
  and cut into quarters
6 egg yolks

Tart—Almonds are a natural addition to this dessert, as Marsala has distinctly nutty undertones. Serve with either toasted almond slices or almond cookies crumbled on top.

Tweak—Experiment with the booze you use—this recipe calls for Marsala, which is a Sicilian fortified wine, but you could try it with Prosecco instead.

Put ¼ cup of the Marsala and a quarter of the sugar into a frying pan and bring to a boil over medium heat, stirring to dissolve the sugar. Add the peaches and cook for 5–10 minutes, shaking occasionally to prevent them from catching on the bottom of the pan, until the peaches are soft and the Marsala is syrupy. (If the peaches do catch on the bottom a little it doesn't really matter—this will add color, texture, and flavor.) Divide the peaches among six serving glasses and set aside.

Put a large saucepan of water on to boil. Meanwhile, put the egg yolks and remaining sugar in a mixing bowl and whisk for 5 minutes, until light and creamy. Turn the water down to barely a simmer and place the mixing bowl containing the egg yolk and sugar mixture on top. Continue to whisk, adding the Marsala in a slow, steady stream. Whisk for another 10–15 minutes, until the *zabaglione* has doubled in volume and is the palest of yellows.

Divide the zabaglione between the peach glasses. Serve hot or cold.

#zabaglione

Elderflower ice cream with lemon cookies

The problem with most ice-cream recipes for a lot of home cooks—myself included—is that they tend to be somewhat prohibitive. If you don't have an ice-cream machine then you are generally stuffed. Yes, you can take your ice-cream mix out of the freezer every half-hour to give it a whisk, but not everyone has the time or the patience for such things. This ice cream, happily, requires no churning and no mid-freeze whisking. It only takes 10 minutes to prepare, leaving you plenty of time to make the cookies. And if you're feeling really lazy, you can always just buy those...

Serves 6

2½ cups heavy cream
⅓ cup elderflower cordial
1 cup confectioners' sugar
juice of ½ a lemon

For the cookies

8 tablespoons (1 stick) softened butter
1 heaping cup all-purpose flour
2 tablespoons sugar
zest of 1 lemon

TART—Add a few chunks of preserved ginger to the ice cream.

TWEAK—Following the above format you can make other ice creams—try swapping the elderflower cordial for ⅓ cup pomegranate juice and a good splash of rosewater.

TOMORROW—This recipe makes the right number of cookies for this dish, but you could double up and store them in a tin for a week.

To make the ice cream, tip the cream, cordial, confectioners' sugar, and lemon juice into a large bowl. Whisk until stiff peaks form (the cream should sit up when flicked upward with a whisk). Tip into an ice-cream tub and let set in the freezer for at least 4 hours, or overnight.

To make the cookies, preheat the oven to 350°F. Rub the butter into the flour with your hands until the mixture resembles coarse bread crumbs, then mix in the sugar and lemon zest with a spoon until it forms a stiff dough. Lightly flour a work surface and roll out the dough to about ¼ inch thick. Trim the edges and cut into 12 fingers with a knife and put on a cookie sheet. Bake in the oven for 8–10 minutes, until pale golden and remove. Let cool on a wire rack. (If, like me, you don't have one of these you can use one of the oven racks instead, the idea is to get some air underneath your cookies to help them to crisp up.)

Store the cookies in an airtight container until ready to use, at which point you can serve them alongside a few scoops of elderflower ice cream.

#elderflowericecream

Poached pears

If zabaglione is a summertime dessert, then poached pears are about as wintry as it gets. The list of ingredients is evidence enough—port, cinnamon, and cloves evoke images of red-faced relatives and games of Scrabble. It's Christmas on a plate, without being leaden and constipating, as a traditional Christmas dessert can be.

Serves 6

1¼ cups tawny or LBV (late-bottled vintage) port
3 cups water
2½ cups superfine sugar
juice of ½ a lemon
2 sticks of cinnamon
10 cardamom pods
2 whole star anise
3 cloves
6 underripe pears
scant 1 cup crème fraîche

Put the port, water, sugar, lemon juice, and spices in a large saucepan. Whisk over medium heat to dissolve the sugar and let warm up. Peel the pears, ideally leaving the stalks on (just because they look good) and trim the bottoms off so that the fruit will sit upright.

Slip the pears into the pan and gently poach for 1 hour, with the liquid barely at a simmer. Prod the pears with a knife or skewer; it should meet no resistance. Once cooked through, remove from the poaching liquor and set aside. Turn up the heat and simmer until syrupy and reduced by half. Serve hot or cold with the syrup and crème fraîche.

#poachedpears

Tweak—If you prefer, then omit the alcohol—it works fine without it.

Tomorrow The pears will keep a week or so in a big jar in the refrigerator, and, oddly enough, go very well with blue cheese.

Feeding the flocks

Feeding the flocks

If the previous chapter was about relatively formal food, then this one is more about laid-back entertaining. Those evenings when you have a group of friends round for a casual supper aren't really the time for fancification and fuss. I prefer to cook something that you can stick in the middle of the table for everyone to grab at. Somehow the idea of elegantly plating up individual dishes feels at odds with the mood.

Spices lend themselves particularly well to party food—they seem to get everyone going. The brain releases endorphins when you eat chili—it's a response to the "pain"—and so eating spicy food gives you a natural high. We're not talking about outrageously hot food, which only burns your mouth and kills your taste buds, but a gentle, invigorating heat.

Many of these recipes can be prepared in advance, so that all you have to do last-minute is heat up a couple of things, stick all the bits and pieces on the table, and leave it to your friends to serve themselves. It's hands-on food.

A cheese and beer fondue

You can serve this simply with chunks of baguette or some boiled baby potatoes. Be gentle with the temperature, and constant with the stirring when making this fondue, or you risk splitting the cheese. Once it's ready you'll want to serve it straight away, so get all your chosen accompaniments prepared before you begin cooking.

Serves 8

½ a clove of garlic
4 tablespoons butter
⅓ cup all-purpose flour
2 cups good beer
3½ cups grated Emmental cheese
3½ cups grated sharp cheddar cheese
1 tablespoon English mustard powder, mixed with a little water

serve with any or all of the following:
• 2–3 baguettes
• 3⅓ pounds baby potatoes, cooked
• a big jar of gherkins
• slices of ham, salami, or chorizo
• a big green salad

Rub a large saucepan all over with the garlic clove, discarding it once you have finished. Add the butter to the pan, melt over medium heat, then add the flour and stir to combine. Cook through for a couple of minutes before adding the beer, a splash at a time, stirring until thickened. Once all the beer has been evenly incorporated and the sauce is smooth, simmer for another few minutes.

Add the cheese a handful at a time, stirring constantly, until fully melted and smooth. Finally, add the mustard and continue to cook, stirring, for another few minutes until smooth and glossy.

Serve immediately with your chosen accompaniments.

#beerfondue

TWEAK—For a more traditional fondue, substitute white wine and a little Kirsch for the beer.

Beef chili tacos

The Mexicans have party food mastered. So much of their cuisine seems tailored for informal eating. Enchiladas, burritos, quesadillas—all these American-adopted dishes hum with chili and conversation. The beauty of street food is, I suppose, that it's inherently convivial and slapdash.

Tacos are really just a variation on a theme—as long as you have some sort of meat, a variety of vegetables, and a vehicle with which to eat them, you're set.

Makes 16 tacos

olive oil
3⅓ pounds beef shank, cut into very small cubes
2 red onions, peeled and minced
2 cloves of garlic, peeled and crushed
4 fresh red chilies, deseeded and minced
1 teaspoon smoked paprika
2 cups good strong beer
2 tablespoons tomato paste
1 x 14-ounce can of kidney beans
salt and pepper
16 taco shells
1 iceberg lettuce, finely shredded
1 x 7-ounce jar jalapenos
2¾ cups grated cheddar cheese

For the tomato and avocado salsa
5 tomatoes
2 avocados
1 red onion, peeled
a handful of cilantro
juice of 1 lime
a pinch of sugar

Preheat the oven to 325°F.

Heat a couple of tablespoons of oil in a large saucepan over medium-high heat and brown the meat a handful at a time. (Don't worry about thoroughness—you're not "sealing" it; you're just adding color and flavor.) Once you've browned all the meat, remove it to a bowl and add a drop more oil to the pan. Lower the heat, toss in the onions, garlic, chilies, and smoked paprika, and sauté for a few minutes until slightly softened and colored.

Return the meat to the pan, pour in the beer, and add the tomato paste and kidney beans. Season generously with salt and pepper and stir. Bring to a boil, cover, and cook in the oven for 1½ hours. Remove from the oven, uncover, and simmer for another half-hour over medium heat, stirring occasionally until thickened.

Meanwhile, make the salsa by mincing the tomatoes, avocados, onion, and cilantro. Put in a bowl, add the lime juice and a few glugs of olive oil, and stir to combine. Add the sugar, season with salt and pepper, cover with cling wrap, and refrigerate until needed.

Warm the taco shells according to the package instructions. Serve a big bowl of the chili along with the tacos, salsa, shredded lettuce, jalapenos, cheddar cheese, cold beer, and, if feeling particularly brave, shots of tequila and verdita (see opposite).

#tacos

Tart—Add some rustic little chunks of chorizo to the stew.

Tweak—For a lighter, quicker taco, toss strips of chicken in smoked paprika, chopped cilantro, and lime juice and fry for 5 minutes. Serve instead of the chili.

Tomorrow—Serve any leftover chili with rice or baked potatoes.

Feeding the flocks

How to make verdita:

There's a very cool bar in East London, about the size of a parking space, where they serve this amazing drink called verdita, which you drink as a chaser to tequila. I've seen even the most squeamish nontequila drinkers positively gush after drinking it. To make, simply blend a large bunch of cilantro, about a third of that of mint, a carton of pineapple juice, and three jalapenos. Strain and chill. Serve a shot alongside a shot of tequila.

Five-spice chicken wings

Chinese five-spice is a handy spice mix for the cupboard. Its aromatic qualities transform the simplest cuts of meat into something spectacular, and make your kitchen smell better than the streets of Chinatown. Chicken wings are cheap, too. You can usually find them in supermarkets; otherwise give your nearest butcher a call a day in advance and I imagine he'll practically give them to you (though don't quote me on that).

Serves 10

4 tablespoons Chinese five-spice powder
3–4 teaspoons hot chili powder
4 teaspoons runny honey
4 tablespoons soy sauce
4 tablespoons olive oil
a few drops of sesame oil
salt and pepper
4½–7 pounds chicken wings

Preheat the oven to 400°F.

In a large bowl, mix together the five-spice, chili powder, honey, soy sauce, and olive and sesame oils. Season with salt and pepper and toss in the chicken wings, coating thoroughly. Tip into a roasting pan or two and roast in the oven for 45 minutes to an hour. They'll be cooked in less time if you're desperate to eat, but ideally you'd give them time to get good and sticky. Serve with paper napkins.

#chickenwings

TART—Garnish the wings with shredded green onions and red chilies.

TWEAK—Instead of five-spice, use a couple of tablespoons of crushed Szechuan peppercorns —they make your mouth go numb in the most pleasing of ways.

7-hour pork belly buns with apple sauce

This is a good Saturday-night dish. You can stick it in the oven at lunchtime, go out for the afternoon, and come back to meat that pulls apart majestically and crackling of brittle perfection. It's like a homemade hog roast. It's worth purchasing a utility knife for scoring pork belly—they only cost a few bucks and make slashing the pigskin a breeze.

Serves 10

9 pounds pork belly
salt and pepper
a handful of rosemary sprigs
14 ounces radishes
a good handful of flat-leaf parsley leaves
10 large Kaiser rolls

for the apple sauce
2 large baking apples
scant 1 cup water
1 tablespoon superfine sugar

With a utility knife or your sharpest knife, score the pork belly skin at ¾-inch intervals. Season the skin with a handful of salt and leave for half an hour. (You're trying to extract any excess moisture, which helps get a really crisp crackling.)
  Preheat the oven to 425°F.
  Scatter a roasting pan with the rosemary and a pinch of salt and pepper. Pat the pork skin dry with kitchen towel, and lay the meat, skin-side up, on top of the rosemary. Put in the oven and cook for half an hour. Reduce the heat to 275°F and roast for another 6–7 hours. Remove the pork from the oven and let rest for at least half an hour.
  To make the apple sauce, peel, quarter, and core the apples, and put in a saucepan over medium heat with the water. Cover and cook for 10–15 minutes, until the apples have cooked down and are fluffy. Add the sugar, stir to combine, and take off the heat.
  Finely slice the radishes (this is easily done on the slicey bit of a cheese grater), put in a bowl and mix with the parsley leaves. Remove the crackling from the pork and pull the flesh apart with tongs or a couple of forks. Fill the rolls with the apple sauce, pork belly, and radish and parsley salad, serving the crackling alongside.
  #porkbellybuns

Tart—Forgo the buns and serve the pork belly with roast potatoes and gravy.

Tweak—Replace the radish and parsley salad with some homemade coleslaw (see p.130).

Tomorrow—There will be a considerable amount of rendered fat left in the roasting pan. This will keep for months covered in the refrigerator, and is ideal for roasting potatoes in.

Lamb kebabs

The human race, you've probably noticed, is quite fond of stuffing bits of meat between pieces of bread. At their best, kebabs sit proudly at the top of the sandwich hierarchy—soft, ever-so-slightly pink hunks of lamb prodded generously into soft, warm pita and licked with garlicky mayonnaise and chili. The flatbread here is very easy to make, but by all means buy a few pitas to save time if you like.

Serves 8

1 heaping cup thick plain yogurt
2 cloves of garlic, peeled
  and crushed
juice of 1 lemon
1 teaspoon cumin seeds,
  crushed
2 sprigs of rosemary, needles
  picked and minced
salt and pepper
olive oil
2¼-pound lamb leg off the
  bone, cubed and trimmed of
  fat
a clove of garlic, crushed
5 tablespoons mayonnaise
  (homemade p.164 or bought)

for the flatbreads
1¾ cups strong bread flour
1 cup all-purpose flour
1 teaspoon yeast
1 teaspoon crushed fennel
  seeds
1 teaspoon salt
scant 1 cup warm water
4 tablespoons olive oil
4 tablespoons thick plain yogurt

serve with any or all of
  the following:
• chili sauce
• ½ a small white cabbage,
  finely shredded
• 1 red onion, peeled and sliced
• 2 carrots, grated
• 1 iceberg lettuce, finely sliced

Mix the yogurt, garlic, lemon juice, cumin seeds, and minced rosemary in a bowl. Season with salt and pepper and loosen with a glug of oil. Coat the lamb in the yogurt mixture and let marinate for 1–2 hours. While the lamb marinates, make the flatbreads following the instructions opposite.

Preheat the oven to 425°F. Tip the marinated lamb into a roasting pan in an even layer and put in the oven for 15 minutes. Meanwhile, get a griddle or frying pan hot over medium-high heat and, one at a time, cook the breads for 2 minutes a side, keeping warm in a clean kitchen towel. Turn the heat down a notch if the breads are burning.

Remove the lamb from the oven and rest while you finish off any breads that remain. Stir the crushed garlic through the mayonnaise and serve with your chosen accompaniments. Let your guests fashion their own kebabs, stuffing the breads with the lamb, garlic mayo, chili sauce, and vegetables.

#kebabs

TART—Add a scattering of pomegranate seeds to the kebabs.

TWEAK—You can play around with the spices you add to the flatbread dough. Coriander seeds, cumin, and chili flakes all work well.

TOMORROW—Make coleslaw by mixing any leftover shredded white cabbage, red onion, and carrot with the garlic mayonnaise.

Feeding the flocks

To make the flatbreads

Combine your dry ingredients in a bowl before
adding the water, oil, and yogurt and
mixing together. Knead on a clean, floured
surface until smooth and elastic. Divide
into 8 pieces and roll out the flatbreads
thinly. Let rest for at least half an hour,
separated by sheets of parchment paper.

Roasted pepper, manchego, and smoked paprika salad

It's rather culturally confused, this dish. Made with red bell peppers it looks like the Italian flag and, were you to get rid of the smoked paprika and substitute the manchego for Parmesan, it would be very Italian indeed. Yet, as it stands, it has a distinctly Spanish vibe, and is all the better for it. Hurrah for the European Union!

Serves 8

6 red, yellow, or orange bell peppers
2 cloves of garlic, peeled and sliced
1 teaspoon sweet smoked paprika
olive oil
salt and pepper
4 ounces arugula leaves
7 ounces manchego cheese
a handful of basil leaves

Preheat the oven to 400°F. Cut the peppers in half lengthwise and remove the seeds and stalks. Cut each half in half lengthwise again and place on a baking sheet with a slice of garlic on top of each piece. Sprinkle the smoked paprika over the peppers, drizzle with olive oil, season with salt and pepper, and roast in the oven for 20 minutes.

Lay the peppers on a serving dish and scatter them with the arugula leaves. With a potato peeler, shave the manchego on top, then tear a few basil leaves, and scatter them over that. Drizzle with olive oil and serve.

#roastedpeppersalad

Tart—Lay a few anchovy fillets over the roasted peppers. You could also throw some marinated artichoke hearts in for good measure.

Tweak—If you can't find manchego, use Parmesan instead.

Tomorrow—The peppers will keep well for a couple of days covered in the refrigerator.

Feeding the flocks

Barlow's delicious cilantro salad

This is a fragrant and punchy salad that my friend Nic makes. It's a fantastic accompaniment to so many things—a refreshing side for a chicken stew or curry—but also works well as a simple and palate-cleansing course in its own right.

Serves 6

juice of 1 lime
1 tablespoon fish sauce
salt and pepper
a pinch of sugar
olive oil
7 ounces cilantro
a good handful of cremini mushrooms, finely sliced
4 green onions, washed and finely sliced
1 fresh red chili, deseeded and minced

In a serving bowl, add the lime juice, fish sauce, a pinch or two of salt, a little pepper, sugar, and a glug of olive oil and stir to combine. Taste and add more oil if necessary.

Pick the leaves from the cilantro (a minor hassle but one that is entirely worth it) and wash them if necessary. Make sure they're dry.

When ready to serve, toss the cilantro, mushrooms, onions, and chili through the dressing and serve immediately.

#coriandersalad

TART—Add a generous handful of roughly chopped peanuts to the dressing.

TWEAK—Swap the mushrooms for some minced grapefruit.

Goat curry

Curry is a great party dish. Placed in the middle of the table in a large cauldron, you can let everyone furnish their plates with whatever condiments they want: mango chutney, a cooling raita, some lime pickle. You can find goat in most Caribbean and Indian stores, but if it proves hard to come by, you can always use lamb instead.

Serves 8

2 teaspoons coriander seeds
2 teaspoons fennel seeds
1 teaspoon cumin seeds
2 cloves
2 teaspoons hot chili powder
½ teaspoon cinnamon
3⅓-pound goat leg off the
  bone, cut into chunks
olive oil
2 onions, peeled and sliced
4 cloves of garlic, peeled
  and sliced
4 fresh red chilies, deseeded
  and sliced
2 teaspoons nigella seeds
1 tablespoon tomato paste
2 cups chicken stock
salt and pepper
2 tablespoons thick plain yogurt
2 shallots, peeled and
  thinly sliced
a handful of cilantro,
  roughly chopped

Put a dry frying pan over medium heat and add the coriander, fennel, and cumin seeds, and the cloves. Toast, shaking the pan every now and then, for a minute or two. Transfer to a mortar and pestle and crush to a rough powder. Mix in the hot chili powder and cinnamon and stir to combine. Put the goat in a bowl and coat thoroughly with the rub. Cover with cling wrap and refrigerate until needed. (Ideally you want to leave it for a few hours or overnight, but half an hour is better than nothing.)

Heat a little oil in a large saucepan and fry the onions for a couple of minutes until soft. Add the garlic, chilies, and nigella seeds and stir for another minute before turning up the heat and adding the goat. Stir over medium-high heat for a few minutes until the meat has started to color.

Add the tomato paste and chicken stock, season to taste, and bring to a boil. Cover and lower the heat to a minimum. Let cook gently for an hour and a half. Remove the lid and simmer for another half-hour until thickened.

Meanwhile, heat ¾ inch of oil in a small saucepan over medium-high heat. Drop in the sliced shallot and fry for a minute, until crisp. Remove with a slotted spoon and dry on paper towels.

Take the curry off the heat and stir through the yogurt. Serve topped with the fried shallots and cilantro. I'd favor warm bread with lots of raita as an accompaniment, or the pilaf on p.108.

#goatcurry

TART—Make a fresh apple and mint chutney by processing a peeled and cored baking apple or two with a shallot, a handful of fresh mint, a dollop of yogurt, and a tablespoon of sugar.

TWEAK—If you prefer a creamier curry, only use half the amount of chicken stock and add a can of coconut milk instead.

TOMORROW—This curry keeps well for a couple of days.

Prepping

A lot of cooking comes down to decent preparation. The reason restaurants can operate at such a level of efficiency is because people are there from six in the morning peeling, chopping, slicing, blanching, reducing, julienning, cracking, and whisking. Mercifully, you're not cooking for 100 people and those you are cooking for will most likely only have a choice of one dish.

Nevertheless, the same rules apply. If all the prep is done properly, then the business of cooking—the really fun bit—is easy.

The right knife
Don't be scared of big, sharp knives. You have a much greater chance of doing yourself damage if you're trying to chop an onion with a small, blunt knife—it will slip around and you have less control. Buy yourself a decent chef's knife and look after it. Once you get the hang of it, you'll find chopping much easier.

Discoloration and wilting
Some ingredients need a little TLC. A peeled potato or parsnip should be put straight into water to stop it from browning. Other roots and fruits—pears and apples, for example—need rubbing with lemon juice or dropping into acidulated water (water with a squeeze of lemon) to prevent discoloration.

Delicate herbs—basil, parsley, tarragon, cilantro, and chives—should only be chopped just before use. The sharper your knife, the less chance you have of bruising the herbs, too.

Blanching
In order to keep their color and texture, green vegetables are best cooked at the last minute. You can, however, do them partly in advance by dropping them into salted, boiling water and cooking until still al dente (when they are cooked but still retain a little bite), before draining and plunging into iced water. Then just reheat in butter or oil at the last-minute.

Meat and veg
It probably goes without saying, but don't chop raw meat on the same board or with the same knife as you chop vegetables.

Macerated strawberries

It's amazing how the smallest of tweaks can turn a largely unadorned fruit into something quirky and interesting. Not that there's anything wrong with a simple strawberry, popped straight in the mouth via a quick cream bath. But with a little extra attention these simple berries can be transformed into something that bit more exciting.

Serves 8

5½ cups strawberries
juice of 1 lemon
a good handful of mint leaves
3 tablespoons sugar
pepper

Hull the strawberries and halve or quarter (depending on size), putting them in a mixing bowl as you go. Add the lemon juice and stir to combine.

Pound the mint and sugar together in a mortar and pestle until you have what is essentially green sugar. Add this to the strawberries and mix through well. Cover and leave in the refrigerator for a couple of hours.

Serve with a few good twists of black pepper.

#maceratedstrawberries

Mojito jello

Feeding your friends jello is bound to encourage childish regression. In a good way. Mostly.

Makes 8 jello desserts

4 cups soda water
3 x ¼-ounce envelopes
  granulated gelatin
a big bunch of fresh mint,
  plus a few sprigs for
  decorating
8 tablespoons superfine sugar
1¾ cups white rum
juice of 4 limes
1 lime, finely sliced

Pour ⅓ cup of the soda water into a small saucepan, sprinkle with the gelatin, and let soak for 5–10 minutes. Meanwhile, in a large saucepan, briefly bash together the bunch of mint and sugar, then pour in the rum, lime juice, and the rest of the soda water. Stir to dissolve the sugar and bring to just under a boil. Remove from the heat and let infuse.

Gently heat the gelatin until melted. Remove the mint from the rum and soda water mixture and slowly pour in the gelatin, whisking as you go. Let cool.

Decant into 8 separate glasses, putting a sprig of mint and a slice of lime in each. Cover and put in the refrigerator to set—6 hours should do it, though allow for longer if you can. Serve when you're ready.

#mojitojelly

Chocolate and fennel brownies

A good brownie recipe is an invaluable thing. They have the ability to lift the blackest of moods—all at once soothing and indulgent. For those eight seconds you spend cramming it into your mouth, the world seems like an all-right place. If serving as a dessert then these are excellent with some good-quality vanilla ice cream, though I'm as fond of them as a snack with a glass of milk.

Makes 24 brownies

1¾ cups (3½ sticks) unsalted butter, cubed
14 ounces semisweet chocolate (minimum 70% cocoa solids), smashed to pieces
6 eggs
2½ cups superfine sugar
1 tablespoon vanilla extract
1¾ cups all purpose flour
2 teaspoons fennel seeds, roughly crushed

Preheat the oven to 350°F. Line a 12-inch x 8-inch x 2-inch baking pan with wax paper. It helps to rub it with the butter wrapper first to make the paper stick.

Put a saucepan of water on to boil and place a heatproof bowl on top. Turn the heat down to low, add the butter and chocolate to the bowl, and let melt. Meanwhile, beat the eggs and sugar together with the vanilla extract until light and pale.

Once melted, cool the chocolate for a few minutes before whisking in the egg mix. Fold in the flour and fennel seeds and scrape into the baking pan. Put in the oven and bake for 25–30 minutes before removing and letting cool.

#brownies

Tart—Add a couple of handfuls of white chocolate buttons to the cake batter before baking. You can also add crushed nuts as well, walnuts being the classic choice.

Tweak—Instead of fennel, add a couple of handfuls of frozen raspberries to the brownie mix.

Tomorrow—These will keep in a tin for a few days, and they also freeze very well.

Lemon grass and basil granita with vodka

While making a proper sorbet requires an ice-cream machine, a granita is an altogether simpler affair. Sure, every now and then you have to give the mixture a prod with a fork, but that only requires all of 30 seconds of your time. If you don't have a measuring cup, then simply use a water glass or something similar—you just need roughly equal volumes of water and sugar.

Serves 8

2 cups superfine sugar
2 cups water
4 stalks of lemon grass,
  roughly chopped
a good handful of basil leaves
juice of 1 lemon
1¾ cups vodka

Put the sugar and water in a saucepan and stir over medium heat until the sugar is fully dissolved. Add the lemon grass and basil, bring to a boil, and simmer for 3 minutes. Remove from the heat, add the lemon juice, and let infuse for 30 minutes as the mixture cools.

Strain into an old ice-cream tub, pyrex dish, or bowl, cover tightly, and put in the freezer along with the vodka. After 1–2 hours remove the granita from the freezer and give it a good whisk with a fork to break up the ice crystals.

Freeze for at least another 4 hours and serve in chilled glasses with the chilled vodka poured over the top.

#lemongrassgranita

TWEAK—If you can't find lemon grass, the zest and juice of 2 lemons and 2 limes makes for a good alternative granita.

Preserves for the pantry

Pickling and preserving remain eternally couched in fusty cliché, which is a terrible shame. Where a sponge cake can perhaps legitimately be seen as "old school" and somewhat unsexy, there's something about the subtle and ancient art of preserving that is quite cool. To be able to casually pluck a jar of pickled beets from your cupboard as a little something to go with pork is inevitably going to impress guests.

Best of all, it's so, so easy. Pickling vegetables is as simple as introducing them to vinegar and sugar, perhaps adding a spice or two along the way just to pep it up a bit. Jams are even simpler, the only caveat being that with some berries you mustn't add the sugar until the fruits have cooked down.

The fact that these preserves and pickles keep so well means that you will always have something interesting to base your dinner on—when stuck for ideas, the realization that you have a jar of onion jam in the cupboard can suddenly provide the inspiration you were lacking. They make fantastic gifts, too, with relatively little effort. In the time it takes you to go shopping you can have made a jar of chutney or pickled cabbage for a loved one, with a little spare for the cupboard. And just how smug-worthy is it to produce a jar of homemade jam as a birthday present?

PICKLING
The sharpness of pickled vegetables lends them best to rich and fatty foods. Just think of the effect a gherkin has on your burger, cutting through the meat's richness and waking your palate. Pâtés and smoked fish are particularly enhanced by the zip of a pickle. Below are a few ideas for pickling, plus suggestions of what you can do with your pickle once it's pickled. I just can't stop saying pickle...

Pickled cucumber

Makes about 2 cups

scant 1 cup white-wine or
  cider vinegar
1½ cups superfine sugar
1 teaspoon fennel seeds
a handful of dill, chopped
  (optional)
1 cucumber
1 onion, peeled and finely sliced
1 teaspoon salt

Pour the white-wine or cider vinegar into a bowl and whisk in the superfine sugar until dissolved. Crush the fennel seeds in a mortar and pestle and add to the pickling liquid with the dill, if using. Finely slice the cucumber (you can use the slicer bit on a grater) and add to the pickling liquid with the chopped onion and salt. Leave for at least an hour before serving, or store in sterilized jars. Aesthetically it's best served sooner rather than later, as it loses its color otherwise, but it will keep for a good while.

#pickledcucumber

✳ To sterilize a jar
Wash the jar thoroughly and leave in the oven at 212°F for half an hour or so.

Lamb chops with pickled cucumber and labneh

Labneh is strained yogurt, like the goat curd on p.98. It makes for a thicker, more cheesy yogurt, while intensifying the yogurt's natural sourness. If you don't have time to make it then just use the thickest yogurt you can find combined with a squeeze of lemon instead.

Serves 4

scant 1 cup plain yogurt
salt and pepper
a clove of garlic, crushed
1 teaspoon chopped rosemary
  needles
juice of ½ a lemon
olive oil
4 thick lamb chops
4 tablespoons pickled cucumber
  (see opposite)
1 tablespoon poppy seeds
  (optional)

To make the labneh, line a strainer with cheesecloth or a clean dish cloth and set in a bowl. Tip in the yogurt, add a pinch of salt, and let strain for between 8 and 48 hours, the longer the better.

Mix together the garlic, rosemary, and lemon juice and combine with a glug of olive oil. Coat the chops in the marinade and leave for an hour or two.

Season the chops with salt and pepper and cook on a hot frying or griddle pan for 4 minutes on each side. Rest for a couple of minutes and serve with the pickled cucumber, labneh, and a scattering of poppy seeds, if you like.

TART—Stir chopped mint, crushed garlic, and grated cucumber through the labneh to make a tzatziki.

TWEAK—This dish works well with goat curd (see p.98) in place of the labneh

Kimchi

This Korean pickled cabbage dish is somewhat different to the other, more traditional pickles listed here, and is highly addictive.

Makes a big jar's worth

4 ounces salt
1 large Chinese or white cabbage
a thumb-sized piece of ginger, peeled and grated
2 cloves of garlic, peeled and minced
a handful of green onions, trimmed and sliced
a handful of juniper berries, gently crushed
2 tablespoons chili powder
⅓ cup rice vinegar
a few shakes of sesame oil
2 tablespoons fish sauce
1 tablespoon sugar

Fill your biggest saucepan with water, add the salt, and stir to dissolve. Slice the cabbage (if using a white cabbage remove the core first) and add to the pan. Place a weighted plate on top so that all the cabbage is submerged, and leave for an hour or two.

Meanwhile, mix together the other ingredients in a bowl.

Drain the cabbage and shake dry. Combine with the other ingredients and put in sterilized jars. Cover tightly and leave at room temperature for a couple of days, until it starts to bubble a little. Store in the refrigerator.

#kimchi

Tart—Serve sprinkled with toasted sesame seeds.
Tweak—Try making this with red cabbage.

Duck breast with kimchi

Serves 2

2 duck breasts
1 tablespoon soy sauce
1 teaspoon runny honey
1 teaspoon grated ginger
1 teaspoon allspice
salt and pepper
olive oil
4 tablespoons *kimchi* (see above)

Take a sharp knife and score the skin-side of the duck breasts at ½-inch intervals. Combine the soy sauce, honey, ginger, and allspice, loosen with a little oil, and coat the duck in it. Let marinate for at least a few hours.

Shake off any excess marinade and rub the duck dry. Season with salt and pepper. Get a little oil hot in a frying pan over medium-high heat and carefully add the duck, skin-side down. Leave for 10 minutes, keeping a close eye on the temperature. Turn and cook for another 5 minutes, brushing the skin-side with the marinade. When you turn the duck the skin will be fairly blackened—this is fine.

Remove from the pan and rest for 5 minutes. Slice the duck thickly and serve with the *kimchi*.

Pickled radishes

Makes a few jars' worth

1 cup white-wine vinegar
3 tablespoons superfine sugar
2 cloves
1 pound 2 ounces radishes,
  halved

Put the vinegar, superfine sugar, and cloves into a saucepan and bring to a boil, stirring to dissolve the sugar. Lower the heat to a simmer. Add the radishes to the pan, turn off the heat, and let cool. Store in sterilized jars.

A crisp salad of chicory, pickled radishes, and apple

Serves 4

2 heads of green chicory
½ a red onion, peeled and very
  finely sliced
4 ounces pickled radishes
  (see above)
a bunch of cilantro
a handful of mint leaves
juice of ½ a lime
1 tablespoon fish sauce
3 tablespoons peanut oil
a pinch of sugar
salt and pepper
1 apple

Wash the chicory and remove the outer leaves. What you do next is up to you—you can either pull the lettuce apart and serve the leaves whole, tear the leaves by hand, or slice the as thick or thinly as you like. Whatever you choose, keep the leaves in ice water until ready to serve.

Put the red onion and pickled radishes in a bowl and stir to combine. Chop the cilantro and mint and add to the bowl. In a separate bowl, whisk together the lime juice, fish sauce, oil, and sugar and season with salt and pepper.

When ready to serve, thoroughly dry the chicory leaves and add to the radishes and onion before grating in the apple. Toss through the dressing and serve immediately.

#pickledradish

Tart—Add some raw grated kohlrabi to this salad. Kohlrabi is a relation of the cabbage, but is milder and sweeter.

Pickled beets

Makes a few jars' worth

1 pound 2 ounces beets
1¼ cups white-wine or
 tarragon vinegar
1¾ cups superfine sugar
2 shallots, finely sliced

Boil the beets in lightly salted water until easily skewered with a knife, this could take 20 minutes to an hour, depending on the size of your beets. Drain and let cool. Rub the cooled beets with your thumb to remove the skin and chop into strips, slices, or cubes. Put the white-wine or tarragon vinegar in a saucepan and add the superfine sugar and sliced shallot. Stir to dissolve the sugar, bring to a boil, and simmer for 3 minutes. Pour over the beets and let cool. Store in sterilized jars.

Smoked trout and pickled beets with horseradish

Serves 4

7 ounces smoked trout
5 ounces pickled beets
 (see above)
2 ounces watercress
4 teaspoons creamed
 horseradish
juice of ½ a lemon
olive oil
salt and pepper

Break up the smoked trout into flakes by hand and arrange on a plate with the pickled beets, watercress leaves, and horseradish. Add the lemon juice, a drizzle of olive oil, and season with salt and pepper. Serve immediately.

#pickledbeetroot

TART—Turn this into an elegant little appetizer or make into canapés by serving on store bought blinis.

TWEAK—Substitute smoked mackerel for the trout.

PRESERVING
Preserves such as these serve a similar purpose to pickles, in that their role is one of cutting through rich food. But chutneys and the like are somehow especially comforting and wintry. They require more time and effort than other pickled vegetables, but once the smell of onions softly cooking in vinegar and wine pervade your kitchen, you'll understand it was worth the extra work.

Onion jam

This makes a couple of jars' worth of jam, but if you want to make a lot then the ingredients all double up neatly enough, though it will require a longer cooking time.

Makes a couple of jars

10 tablespoons butter
5 large onions, peeled and finely sliced
½ cup + 2 tablespoons superfine sugar
1 teaspoon salt
pepper
½ a bottle of red wine
⅓ cup cider vinegar

Melt the butter in a saucepan over medium heat and, swishing the pan occasionally, allow it to color gently until nutty brown. You'll need to keep a close eye on it. When a light chestnut color, stir in the onions, sugar, and salt and season with pepper. Stir to coat the onions, turn the heat down to low, and cover with a lid. Let cook for 1 hour, stirring occasionally.

Remove the lid and add the red wine and cider vinegar. Turn the heat up to medium and simmer for another 45 minutes to an hour, stirring occasionally until thick and sticky. Let cool and store in sterilized jars.

#onionjam

Onion jam and goat cheese toasts

Serves 2

2 slices of bread or brioche
2 tablespoons onion jam
4 ounces goat cheese

Preheat the broiler to high. Lightly toast the bread or brioche slices. Spread them with the onion jam and top with a generous wedge of goat cheese. Place under the broiler for 2 minutes. Serve with a handful of dressed salad greens.

START—Little versions of these toasts would make great canapés.

Tasting and seasoning

We are told to be wary of eating too much salt, and so I'll preface this by saying that it is entirely up to you how much you season your food.

 Salt is a life-giving force. Not only could we not survive without it, but food without salt is bland and flat. It is a flavor enhancer, and what is cooking if not an exercise in getting a few ingredients to taste as good as possible together?
 So season intelligently. Taste your food, and season when necessary. As a rule of thumb there are two times to add salt: at the beginning of cooking and at the end. Throwing in salt at the beginning, when there's no need to use your best flaky sea salt which dissolves anyway, adds depth and means it is distributed throughout the dish and absorbed into the ingredients. Added at the end, when the pleasing crunch of sea salt flakes is more appropriate, it is more raw, prominent, and mouthwatering. How much you add depends entirely on how salty the dish already is. Sometimes you'll only need the merest pinch. Other times you'll need considerably more.
 Give some thought to what other ingredients are already there. Certain foods are naturally salty—anchovies, Parmesan, feta, nuts, bacon, stock cubes—so take care before you season.
 Cut meat almost always needs finishing with salt—just a pinch makes all the difference to a carved piece of chicken. A few flakes of sea salt on a resting steak lift it enormously.
 Pepper is important too—proper freshly ground pepper, as opposed to the stale-tasting ready-ground sneezing powder. While salt enhances flavor, pepper gives it bite and edge. I'd also include sharp, acidic ingredients in the seasoning bracket—lemon juice or vinegar is often what is needed when something feels lackluster. With rich foods in particular their acidity wakes up the palate and cuts through the fat, a buttery sauce such as hollandaise given pep and zing by the addition of lemon.
 Taste your food and follow your instincts. All you need to remember is that it's much easier to add something than it is to take it away.

Tomato and chili jelly

This jelly is good with cold meats of any description. Slathered in a ham sandwich it transforms something very simple into a spectacular lunch. A gamey terrine is much improved with this accompaniment. It's important to use preserving sugar here, as it makes for a clearer jelly.

Makes a few jars' worth

2¼ pounds tomatoes, halved
2 red chilies, roughly chopped
1 lemon, sliced
1¾ cups water
scant 1⅔–2¼ cups preserving
  sugar

Put the tomatoes in a large saucepan with the red chilies, lemon, and water. Bring to a boil, cover, and gently simmer for about half an hour. Let cool. Line a large bowl with a clean cheesecloth or clean dish cloth and add the tomatoes. Bringing the corners of the cheesecloth together, tie it up with string, and then hang it from a cupboard handle over the bowl. Leave for at least 6 hours, or preferably overnight.

Measure the clear juices in the bowl and pour into a saucepan with scant 1⅔ cups preserving sugar for every 2 cups of juice, or thereabouts. Put over medium heat and stir until the sugar dissolves. Bring to a boil and boil (note *boil*, not simmer) for about half an hour, skimming off any scum that rises to the top. To test if the jelly is ready, put a teaspoon of it on a plate in the refrigerator for a couple of minutes. If it wrinkles when prodded, then it's ready; if not, boil it for a little longer.

Let cool for 20 minutes before pouring into sterilized jars. It will keep for several months.

#tomatoandchillijelly

Rhubarb and ginger chutney

Pork and rhubarb are an excellent marriage, making this chutney a good match with pork chops and mashed potatoes. Use it instead of the apple sauce for the pork belly buns on p.129.

Makes a few jars' worth

4 tablespoons butter
2 onions, peeled and chopped
salt and pepper
a thumb-sized piece of ginger,
  peeled and grated
1¾ pounds rhubarb, chopped
1¾ cups superfine sugar
a wineglass of red wine
a wineglass of red-wine vinegar

Melt the butter in a large saucepan and toss in the chopped onions. Season with salt and pepper and soften over lowish heat for 10 minutes or so. Add the grated ginger, rhubarb, sugar, wine, and red-wine vinegar and stir to dissolve. Bring to a boil, cover, and leave over moderate heat for 15 minutes. Remove the lid and cook for another 45 minutes, stirring occasionally, until thickened and reduced. Let cool and store in sterilized jars.

#rhubarbchutney

SOUSING
In an otherwise vegetarian chapter it might seem odd to suddenly stick in a random fish recipe, but pickled fish is an outrageously delicious thing to have tucked up your sleeve. While preserving meat entails a fair amount of finesse and waiting around, oily fish like anchovies, sardines, and herring can be pickled and jarred with much greater ease. This recipe is for soused mackerel, but the pickle can be applied to any of the fish mentioned above.

Soused mackerel

The natural partner to this is horseradish: nostril-clearing and punchy enough to cut through the alcohol edge of the sousing liquor.

Makes a big jar's worth
a good handful of salt
2 cups water
8 mackerel fillets
1 heaping cup cider vinegar
⅓ cup vodka
1 bay leaf, finely sliced
a small handful of juniper
    berries, lightly crushed
2 shallots, peeled and
    finely sliced
pepper

Mix the salt and the water in a bowl until the salt has dissolved, and pour the brine over the mackerel fillets in a dish of some description. Leave for a couple of hours.
    Meanwhile, boil the vinegar, vodka, bay leaf, juniper berries, and shallot in a saucepan for 2 minutes, before letting cool.
    Drain the mackerel and discard the salty water. Pat the fillets dry. When the sousing liquor has cooled entirely, pour it into a sterilized jar and slide in the mackerel. Season with pepper, seal tightly, and leave in the refrigerator for at least 3 days before serving. It should keep for a few weeks.
    #sousedmackerel

JAMMING

You can buy so many wonderful jams these days that we often forget how simple they are to make yourself. Even in the depths of winter, frozen berries are easy to come by and are a good way of making the morning toast more exciting. Few things are more reassuring than the sound and smell of jam bubbling gently on the stove. I've used frozen fruits for this recipe—they're a great resource in winter months and, where the idea of pitting 2¼ pounds of cherries is enough to put a lot of people off making jam, using frozen berries bypasses this issue. By all means use fresh berries if you like.

Cherry jam
Makes a few jar's worth

2¼ pounds fresh or frozen
  cherries
juice and zest of 2 lemons
2 cups superfine sugar

Put the cherries in a saucepan with the lemon juice and zest. Put over medium heat, cover, and simmer for 30 minutes, stirring occasionally until they have cooked down and softened. Stir in the superfine sugar and bring to a boil. You want to pitch the heat somewhere between a simmer and a full-on boil. It should be bubbling away quite merrily. Boil for 30 more minutes, stirring occasionally to prevent burning. To check if the jam is done, put a little of the juice on a plate and stick in the refrigerator for a couple of minutes. If the jam wrinkles when prodded then it's done. Remove from the heat and cool for 30 minutes before transferring to sterilized jars.

#cherryjam

TWEAK—To make a blueberry jam, follow the same recipe but substitute blueberries for the cherries, adding a good glug of *crème de cassis* along with the sugar.

TART—To add an earthy, herbal flavor to your jam, add a bay leaf to the saucepan with the cherries and lemon juice.

Cherry bakewell tart

Serves 6-8

1 x basic piecrust pastry recipe
  (p.178), or 10 ounces ready-
  made piecrust pastry
3 tablespoons cherry jam
  (see opposite)
8 tablespoons (1 stick) softened
  butter
½ cup superfine sugar
2 eggs
scant 1 cup ground almonds
1 tablespoon all-purpose flour
salt
a small handful of sliced
  almonds (optional)
1 tablespoon confectioners'
  sugar

Line a 12-inch tart pan with the pastry and blind-bake as per the instructions on p.179. Let cool for a few minutes. Spread the bottom of the base with a generous pasting of cherry jam. Cream the butter and sugar together until pale and fluffy, and then beat in the eggs, one at a time. Fold in the ground almonds and flour and add a pinch of salt.

Spread this mixture over the jam and put in the oven at 350°F. Bake for 45 minutes and cool before serving with sliced almonds and a dusting of confectioners' sugar.

#bakewelltart

Drop scones

Makes 6 scones

1 heaping cup self-rising flour
a pinch of salt
1 tablespoon superfine sugar
2 eggs
⅔–scant 1 cup whole milk
sunflower oil

What I love about batter-based dishes such as this is that they are nearly impossible to screw up. The magical combination of flour, eggs, and milk will always produce something pancake-y, and from there you can tweak with abandon.

Sift the flour into a clean bowl and add a pinch of salt and the sugar. Make a well in the middle and drop in the eggs. Slowly pour in the milk, whisking as you go, until the mixture comes together and forms a smooth batter.

Preheat the oven to 140°F. Rub a frying pan with a little sunflower oil and put over moderate heat. Add 2 teaspoons of the mixture to the pan and cook until bubbles start to appear on the surface. Turn it over and cook for another minute. (It's worth doing just one scone to start with, until you get the temperature right, then go on doing a few at a time, keeping the done scones warm in the oven.)

Serve with blueberry or cherry jam (see opposite) and butter or clotted cream.

#dropscones

Preserves for the pantry

BOOZING
Adding flavor to moonshine is an ancient and superb way of transforming cheap grog into something sweet, satisfying and, when consumed in larger quantities than is wise, inebriating. It's a fun thing to do—usually simple, though on occasion, time-consuming. Sloe gin, for example, requires painstaking pricking of the small berries and months, even years, of waiting for your final tipple to reach its peak. These drinks are quicker to make, albeit not always immediately ready to drink.

Toffee vodka

Though the method is unconventional, the heat of the dishwasher is enough to melt the toffee and infuse the vodka with its own unique flavor.

Makes a bottle's worth

1 x 1-liter bottle of vodka
2 ounces Werther's Original, or other hard-boiled toffee candy

Decant the vodka into a pitcher. Roughly chop or blend your toffee candy in a food processor and tip into the empty bottle. Pour enough vodka in to fill the bottle and close tightly. Put the bottle in the top of a dishwasher and set it on a cycle. Once done, strain the vodka through cheesecloth or a dish cloth into another bottle, and chill.

#toffeevodka

Chili vodka

This is not a drink to be taken on its own, unless you are particularly in need of an inferno in your mouth. Instead, it's a good replacement for Tabasco in a Bloody Mary, and even works in a chili con carne or a beef consommé.

Makes a bottle's worth

2 fresh red chilies, halved and deseeded (see p.23)
1 x 1-liter bottle of vodka

Drop the halved chilies into the bottle of vodka, seal, and leave for 8 weeks. Patience, my friend.

#chillivodka

Rhubarb vodka

This one also requires a certain level of patience. Drink it either very cold as a digestif, or use as a base for a cocktail—a rhubarb martini, for example.

Makes a bottle's worth

4 sticks of rhubarb
1 cup superfine sugar
juice of 1 lemon
1 clove
1 x 1-liter bottle of vodka

Slice the rhubarb into 1-inch chunks and roughly mash to a pulp with a wooden spoon in a large mixing bowl, or briefly blend in a blender. Put the mixture into a 1-liter jar, add the clove, and pour the vodka over. Shut tightly and leave in a cool, dark place for a month, shaking daily if possible. After a month, pass through a cheesecloth-lined funnel into bottles. Leave for another month before drinking.

#rhubarbvodka

Preserves for the pantry

Surfing the stumbling blocks

Surfing the stumbling blocks

There are certain dishes that carry with them a mythical and revered hush of ruined dinner parties and distraught cooks. The image of a sweaty and flour-covered hostess weeping over a fallen soufflé is a familiar one, while a decent hollandaise sauce seems to be the perceived Everest of the home cook.

Some of these dishes are viewed as such for a good reason —the margin for error is not vast. It's not like making, say, a stew, whereby you can throw the various ingredients in a pot and, with enough seasoning and time, there isn't much that can go too far wrong. These dishes do require care and attention. But they are far from the panic-inducing behemoths they are frequently made out to be. In fact, I often find, particularly when using eggs, that the more relaxed you are, the more likely things are to go well.

All that is required is a deep breath, good preparation, and a little concentration. I believe this so strongly that there are no tricks in this chapter—no "what they didn't tell you about a soufflé," or secret Freemason's recipe for a poached egg. Of course, there are things to keep in mind when making these dishes—for soufflé think "air" for mayonnaise think "slow," and for roast chicken think...well, actually you don't need to think much. Just stick it in the oven and leave it there for an hour.

At the risk of making this sound like a self-help book, these kinds of recipes do hang, to an extent, on your frame of mind. If you are tearing about the kitchen in the most magnificent state of anxiety, then it's no wonder your dinner refuses to behave. Cooking's no fun that way at any rate. Read the recipe, maybe read it again, get your gear and ingredients together, and trust yourself to do it right.

Mayonnaise and other emulsions

Emulsions involve incorporating one ingredient into another. In a basic salad dressing you want to emulsify the oil and vinegar (and often mustard). You know when it looks like there are drops of oil in the vinegar? That's because the dressing hasn't emulsified. In this case it's no big deal; you just have less consistent flavor in the sauce.

The thing to remember with a mayonnaise is that your only enemy is yourself. Keep a cool head, take your time, and you will have the most perfect pale, wobbly mayonnaise in 5 minutes.

How to make mayonnaise

Put a sturdy bowl on a crumpled-up kitchen towel—this stops it from sliding around—and add two EGG YOLKS, a pinch of SALT, and half a teaspoon of MUSTARD. Give it a little whisk. In a measuring cup—or any old cup—combine roughly ⅓ cup of OLIVE OIL and ⅓ cup of SUNFLOWER or VEGETABLE OIL. Absolutely no need to be scientific about this. Now whisk the oil into the eggs, a drop at a time. Once the mixture starts to thicken you can speed up, but only a little, pouring the oil in a steady and gentle stream and whisking as you go. If the mayonnaise ever looks like it's thinking about splitting then slow down with the oil. Keep going until it's all gone. Whisk in a good squeeze of lemon juice and there you go. Easy.

#mayonnaise

How to tart up your mayonnaise
• Add chopped capers, gherkins, shallot, and parsley for a tartar sauce.
• Add chopped egg, gherkins, capers, parsley, and tarragon for a sauce gribiche.
• Crushed garlic added to mayonnaise makes an aioli.
• Saffron added to aioli makes a *rouille*—a classic dressing for a fish soup.
• Minced chilies and parsley added to aioli makes an excellent dip for broiled shrimp.
• Stir some pesto through the mayonnaise for a good accompaniment to broiled chicken.
• Combine with ketchup and minced gherkin and caper for a thousand-island dressing.
• Stir in some grainy mustard for *Dijonnaise*.

If your emulsion does split, then all is not lost. In a separate bowl, whisk a single egg yolk and add the split mixture a drop at a time, whisking as you go. Once you've added this, continue adding any oil or butter as before.

Warm emulsions

Once you've grasped the principles of mayonnaise then you should be able to make a warm emulsion such as a hollandaise sauce easily. The most important thing to remember is heat control, which, using the below method, is fairly straightforward. Make sure you have every other element of the dish ready to serve before making the sauce, as it's best not to leave a warm emulsion sitting around.

How to make hollandaise

Melt 10 tablespoons of BUTTER in a small saucepan. Don't worry about the white bits in the butter; these are milk solids and, although some recipes recommend skimming them off, I find adding them to the sauce enriches it and loosens it up.

Bring a pan of water to a boil, turn right down to below a simmer, and set a heatproof bowl on top. The bowl shouldn't touch the water. Whisk two EGG YOLKS with a pinch of SALT in the bowl until it streaks the side of the bowl. Remove from the pan and add the melted butter in a gentle trickle, whisking continuously. If it ever looks like splitting add a drop of COLD WATER. When the butter has been fully incorporated, whisk in a squeeze of LEMON JUICE and serve immediately with fish, steamed asparagus, or Eggs Benedict (see p.172).

#hollandaise

How to tart up your hollandaise

• Make your hollandaise into a Béarnaise sauce by first softening shallots in some olive oil and tarragon vinegar. Strain the vinegar into your bowl, add the egg yolks, and proceed as above. Finish with chopped tarragon and, if possible, chervil.
• Cold ham and beef are delicious with a bavaroise sauce —hollandaise with a pinch of chopped thyme and a blob of horseradish added to it.
• For a full coronary, fold 4 tablespoons of whipped cream into the hollandaise for a mousseline. A (slightly) lighter version of this is a *crème fleurette* sauce, which is hollandaise with crème fraîche folded through it.
• Roughly chop sorrel and wilt it in a medium-hot frying pan with a little water, before stirring it through the hollandaise. Heavenly with fish.

A white sauce

This is probably the first thing that Eileen Buchanan, the brave lady who took me on as a student for a week when I was 14, taught me. It might seem old-fashioned, but it's a handy sauce to have a grasp of. It uses a roux—the butter and flour bit—to thicken it, which is a good base for other dishes. When making a roux you don't need to be too finicky about quantities, but I've been precise just to give you an idea of what you're aiming at.

How to make a white sauce

Warm 2 cups of WHOLE MILK until steaming in a saucepan. Meanwhile, melt 2 tablespoons of BUTTER in another pan until bubbling and stir in 2 tablespoons of FLOUR. Stir for a couple of minutes to cook out the flour, and then add the milk, a splash at a time, stirring to thicken. Season with SALT and PEPPER (white pepper if you're being prissy), gently simmer for 10 minutes or so, and use as you wish.

#whitesauce

What to do with your white sauce

A roux is useful for thickening sauces and gravies. You can make a batch of it, which will keep in the refrigerator for a couple of weeks.

After that, the white "mother sauce" can be tarted up and used for masses of other dishes. Even just a grating of nutmeg makes for a soothing accompaniment to fish. Otherwise you can use it for:

❋ Lasagne

A simple white sauce, or *béchamel*, provides the creamy bit for a lasagne, a recipe for which I don't think I need to add to an already groaning canon.

❋ Croque-monsieur, Croque-madame

Preheat the broiler. Lightly toast a couple of pieces of BREAD and spread with WHITE SAUCE. Top with slices of HAM and CHEESE and pop under the broiler until brown and bubbling. Finish with a FRIED EGG for a croque-madame.

✳ Cheese Sauce
Throw a big handful of CHEDDAR CHEESE or GRUYÈRE into your WHITE SAUCE and you have the sauce for macaroni cheese. Spoon the same sauce over white fish and bake in the oven for a classic "mornay."

✳ Parsley Sauce
Pretty straightforward, this one. Add a big handful of chopped PARSLEY and a squeeze of LEMON to a white sauce. Good old-school condiment for ham or white fish.

✳ Soufflé
A cheese soufflé (see p.181) uses a white sauce as its base.

Surfing the stumbling blocks

Eggs, Eggs, Eggs

Before starting this chapter I chatted to various friends, both "real" and "virtual" (i.e. Twitter) about what most intimidated them in the kitchen. It was interesting to find that eggs featured in many of these recipes. Eggs misbehave. It's why emulsions can go wrong, and why soufflés don't always quite work. It almost always comes down to the egg—or at least your treatment of the egg.

If the temperature is wrong (another vital factor) then it is the egg that will rebel first. If you over- or underwhisk the egg white then it can collapse. Buy the freshest and highest quality eggs you can, cook with care, and there shouldn't be any problems.

How to make an omelet

Beat three EGGS thoroughly with a tablespoon of MILK and season with SALT and PEPPER.

Put a small frying pan or omelet pan over medium-high heat and add 2 tablespoons of BUTTER. Melt until foaming and pour in the eggs. With a heatproof spatula, work around the edge of the pan, pulling the eggs away from the sides while pouring, so that the eggs in the middle swish around the now-exposed edge. Do this twice around, then let the omelet sit there for 30–40 seconds, until the top is almost set.

Remove from the heat and tip onto a plate, letting gravity fold the omelet over as you go. Serve immediately.

#omelette

⇒ A Cheese Omelet

Perhaps the simplest variation on a theme, all you need do is toss in a handful of GRATED CHEESE when the OMELET is sitting for 30 seconds.

⇒ A Mixed Herb Omelet

Add minced fresh FLAT-LEAF PARSLEY, CHERVIL, TARRAGON, and CHIVES to the egg mixture at the beginning. For a simpler herby omelet, just add chopped fresh PARSLEY.

How to make scrambled eggs

There are varying theories on how to make the best scrambled eggs. Some favor the quick hot technique, while others go for a slower, more meditative method of scrambling eggs. The texture of the finished product is contingent on which you choose—hot and fast leads to more scrambly scrambled eggs, if you follow, while the long, slow method gives you creamier eggs that fall in drifts.

I favor the slow method, in that it gives you more time to wander about the kitchen doing other things, and also means the temperature of the pan never gets hot enough for them to overcook much once you take them off the stove. Fast, hot eggs will be inedible 15 minutes after cooking, while slow eggs will not. Nevertheless, if you are in a hurry, then by all means opt for the quick method, stirring almost constantly and taking care not to overcook.

Melt 1 tablespoon of BUTTER over low heat and drop in 2–3 fresh EGGS. Season with SALT and PEPPER and stir to break up. Cook for 8–10 minutes, stirring regularly, until soft and creamy. Serve immediately.

How to make a poached egg

Bring a pan of water to a boil. Add a dash of WHITE-WINE VINEGAR. Break the freshest EGG you can find into an espresso cup or something similar. Gently swirl the water in the pan to create a sort of whirlpool and drop the egg into the center. Turn the heat down and leave the egg for 3 minutes. Remove with a slotted spoon and briefly sit on paper towels (the egg, not you) before serving.

If you're doing more than 1 egg, then as long as your eggs are super-fresh, you should be fine. I wouldn't attempt more than 4 at a time, however. Instead, do them in batches, plunging them briefly into cold water as soon as they're cooked to prevent any further cooking.

Poached duck egg with baby potatoes and lovage

I recommend the use of waxy baby potatoes for this salad, as they are deliciously buttery. This works either as an appetizer or as a light supper.

Serves 2

10 ounces baby potatoes
salt and pepper
olive oil
2 green onions, trimmed and
   sliced at an angle
a few lovage leaves, chopped
4 tablespoons butter
white-wine vinegar
2 duck eggs
a few chive flowers (optional)

Wash the potatoes and cut them into smallish pieces. Put in a pan of salted water and bring to a boil. Simmer until yielding to the prod of a knife—about 7 minutes should do it—and drain.

Heat a little oil in a frying pan and gently fry the green onions until softened. Add the potatoes, lovage, and butter and season with salt and pepper. Cover to keep warm.

Meanwhile, put another pan of water (with a splash of vinegar) on to boil for the eggs. Swirl the water, gently drop in the eggs, and poach for 4 minutes. Remove with a slotted spoon and dry on paper towels. Serve the potatoes with the duck eggs and garnish with a few chive flowers, if you like.

#poachedduckeggsalad

Tart—A few slices of salty Serrano or prosciutto would be lovely, particularly if serving as an entree. A few crispy bacon slices would work well, too.

Tweak—You could, of course, use hens' eggs rather than ducks, poaching them for a minute less. Lovage is quite an acquired taste, so if feeding fussy eaters then use chopped parsley instead.

On making mistakes

Home cooking is not a science. Well, let me put it differently. The home kitchen is not a laboratory, and so, by extension, home cooking is not a science. Don't get me wrong—the act of cooking itself is a science, most definitely. You're taking various elements and changing their state through heat, freezing, breaking down, and combining. It's science undoubtedly. But your level of control is limited at home, and so there is no way of knowing exactly how something will turn out.

Things will go awry. The oven might not be behaving as it's meant to. Perhaps you didn't set it right or you put the food on the wrong shelf. Or maybe it's a particularly humid day and your pastry got too warm or wet. Or maybe you were just tired, distracted, rushing, and did something you weren't supposed to. We all do it.

Weights, measurements, temperatures, and cooking times—these are rarely precise in the home. Cookers, pan sizes, measuring cups, scales, and ovens all have varying levels of accuracy and reliability. It's better to be conscious of these things and judge for yourself or learn through trial and error rather than get too bogged down in the detail.

Remember that this isn't television and you aren't being judged. It's dinner. If things don't go exactly according to plan then it's likely that no one will even notice. I was once making truffles for a dinner party I'd been drafted in to cater. I added a shake of chili powder to the mix and carried on with the truffles. I'd done this a hundred times, and thought I knew exactly what I was doing. Before serving them I popped one in my mouth, as you do. Something had gone wrong. They tasted bizarre. Looking more closely at the jar of "mild chili powder," I found it to contain oregano, cumin, and garlic. Channeling Heston I served them anyway. No one noticed.

It's very easy to live or die by the success of a meal, and of course it's frustrating when something you've spent time on misfires. But really, the best thing to do is laugh and get on with it. Eat some toast. Drink more wine. Ultimately, this is just food.

Eggs Benedict

A classic breakfast, you can serve this with smoked ham, smoked fish, or, as in this case, crispy bacon. It can be a bit of a juggling act, so make sure you have all your ingredients measured and ready before you begin.

Serves 2

4 strips of smoked bacon
4 fresh eggs, broken into 4
  espresso cups or similar
white-wine vinegar
2 English muffins, homemade
  (see p.82) or store-bought,
  halved

For the hollandaise
6 tablespoons warm melted
  butter
1 large or 2 small egg yolks
juice of ½ a lemon
salt

Put a frying pan over medium heat and gently fry the bacon until crisp. Keep warm until needed.

To make the hollandaise, bring a pan of water to a boil. Turn the heat down to barely a simmer and sit a heatproof mixing bowl on top. Add the 2 egg yolks and whisk for 30 seconds to a minute, until the eggs start to leave streaks on the bowl. Remove the bowl and whack the pan back up to a boil, adding a splash of vinegar as you do. Start very slowly whisking the melted butter into the egg yolks. Once the pan of water is boiling again, carefully drop in the 4 poaching eggs, one by one. Poach for 3 minutes as you continue to whisk the hollandaise, finishing it with a squeeze of lemon and a pinch of salt.

Toast the muffins, remove the eggs from the water with a slotted spoon, and dry on paper towels if necessary. Butter, the muffins, if you like, and top each with the fried bacon, a poached egg, and hollandaise.

#eggsbenedict

Roasting a chicken

Out of all the dishes people seem to find most intimidating and difficult to perfect, roast chicken seems to be a consistent *bête noire*. This is odd, considering that it is difficult to screw up. The following recipe serves four but of course, if you're feeding more you'll need a bigger bird. Cook it for 40 minutes per 2¼ pounds, giving it a decent rest at the end of cooking.

How to roast chicken

Preheat the oven to 425°F. Rub a 3⅓-pound CHICKEN all over with 4 tablespoons of BUTTER and season with SALT and PEPPER. Cut a LEMON in half and squeeze the juice over the chicken, before stuffing the halves into the cavity with a handful of THYME SPRIGS and a halved bulb of GARLIC.

Put in the oven and roast for 15 minutes. Turn the heat down to 375°F and roast for another 45 minutes. Remove from the oven and rest in a warm place. You could loosely lay a sheet of foil on top, but don't cover it tightly or you'll soggy up your lovely crisp skin.

#roastchicken

Things to bear in mind

There are two vital and often overlooked aspects to this dish. First, it's essential that you take the chicken out of the refrigerator at least an hour before cooking—preferably two. It needs to be room temperature when it goes in the oven; otherwise it's going to skew your timing.

Second, you should let it rest in a warm place for at least 15 minutes before serving—ideally half an hour. Chicken that seems dry and overcooked is often only so because it has been carved hot out of the oven, the flesh all at once losing its juiciness and drying as the hot meat meets cold air. The best thing about the resting part is that it gives you plenty of time to finish your vegetables and make gravy.

And don't feel you have to make 17 different vegetable sides. A few roast potatoes are lovely, of course, and buttery carrots a happy accompaniment, but there's no need to go overboard. A chicken is a thing of beauty in itself, and is often best eaten simply with gravy, a few baby potatoes, and a green salad. As for the chicken itself, well, this isn't a crusading book, but you get what you pay for.

Surfing the stumbling blocks

TART—Play about with the seasonings on a very basic level, swapping the thyme for tarragon or rosemary, or laying a few strips of bacon over the breasts.

TWEAK—Cream the soft butter with chopped thyme, parsley, garlic, and lemon zest and carefully push under the chicken skin, spreading over the meat with your fingers. Roast as before.

TOMORROW—Turn any leftover roast chicken into a Wasabi Chicken Salad (see p.177).

Gravy

Often, when at my most lazy, I won't bother to make gravy, preferring instead to scoop the lemony, garlicky juices from the pan. But for a proper Sunday roast it is pretty essential. Here are the best two ways of making gravy.

The flour method (for a thicker gravy)
Remove your chicken to a carving board or plate, and put the roasting pan over medium-high heat. If there is a lot of fat in the pan pour some of it off, but take care not to lose the lovely meat juices. Add a heaped tablespoon of FLOUR to the pan and stir for a couple of minutes, as if making a roux (see p.166), scraping the meat juices from the bottom of the pan. Add about 2 cups of CHICKEN STOCK, slowly at first, and simmer for 10 minutes, stirring occasionally, until thickened.

The grog method (for a thinner gravy)
Remove the chicken from the pan and let rest on a carving board. Put the roasting pan over high heat and pour in ⅔ cup of white wine or sherry (or Marsala, Madeira, manzanilla, etc). Let it froth and fizz as you scrape the roasting juices from the pan. Simmer and reduce by half. Add 1¼ cups of stock, bring to a boil, and simmer until ready to serve.

To make stock

Simply throw the bones of your roast into a saucepan with any or all of: half an onion, a carrot, a tomato, a stalk of celery, parsley stalks, thyme, a bay leaf, and peppercorns and cover with water. Bring to a boil and skim off any scum that forms on top. Gently simmer for 2–3 hours. Keep in the refrigerator and use within three days.

Pot-roast chicken

This method ensures the juiciest roast chicken imaginable and, as it's cooked with a load of vegetables in the pot, only requires a few boiled baby potatoes alongside. The bonus is that at the end you also have some ready-made chicken stock.

Serves 4

olive oil
8 strips of smoked or unsmoked bacon
2 tablespoons butter
2–3 onions, peeled and chopped
2 stalks of celery, trimmed and chopped
2 leeks, trimmed and sliced
4 large carrots, washed and thickly sliced
3 cloves of garlic, left whole
3 sprigs of thyme, leaves picked
salt and pepper
1¼ cups white wine
1 x 3⅓–4½-pound chicken
6⅓ cups water

In a large saucepan, heat a little oil and fry the bacon until crisp. Add the butter and tumble in the vegetables, garlic, and thyme. Season with salt and pepper, cover, and sweat for 20 minutes, stirring occasionally, until softened. Add the white wine and simmer for a couple of minutes before lowering in the chicken. Pour enough water in to go two-thirds of the way up the chicken, and season the bird with salt and pepper.

Cover, bring to a boil, then simmer over low heat for an hour and a half. Toward the end of the cooking time, preheat the oven to 400°F. When the time comes, take the lid off the pot and put the chicken in the oven for 20 minutes to crisp up the skin.

Remove the chicken from the pan and let rest in a warm place for 20 minutes. Put the pan over gentle heat to keep warm while the chicken rests. Carve the bird and serve with spoonfuls of vegetables and broth.

#potroastchicken

To carve a chicken

With a long, sharp knife, cut down through the join between the leg and breast. Turn the chicken on its side and cut around the joint, sticking to the backbone, removing the leg and thigh together. Repeat on the other side, then carve away the breast meat in thin slices.

Wasabi chicken salad with rice noodles

Leftover roast chicken has to be one of the greatest things to have in your refrigerator—there's so much you can do with it. This salad is punchy and invigorating. You should be able to find wasabi powder in your local grocery store, but if you can't, just leave it out—or grab a package of wasabi paste from your nearest sushi joint instead.

Serves 2–4

10 ounces rice noodles
10 ounces–1⅓ pounds leftover
  roast chicken, stripped from
  the bones
a handful of peanuts,
  roughly chopped
1 fresh red chili, deseeded
  (see p.23) and sliced
a bunch of cilantro
a handful of bean sprouts
2 green onions, trimmed
  and sliced

For the dressing
1 teaspoon wasabi powder
1 tablespoon mirin
1 teaspoon fish sauce
a dash of sesame oil
juice of ½ a lime
sugar
2 tablespoons sunflower oil

Cook the rice noodles according to the package instructions. Meanwhile, make the dressing by mixing the wasabi, mirin, fish sauce, sesame oil, and lime juice together. Add the sugar, whisk in the sunflower oil, and set aside.

Toss together the chicken, noodles, peanuts, chili, cilantro, bean sprouts, and green onions. Spoon the dressing over the salad and serve immediately.

#wasabichickensalad

Piecrust pastry

At its most basic, pastry is a simple combination of flour, butter, and water—usually roughly half the weight of butter to flour, combined until bread crumby and bound with water. From there you can jazz it up with sugar, lemon zest, crushed spices, or egg yolk. Once you get the hang of it, it's a fun and somewhat therapeutic thing to make—and an impressive thing to pull off.

How to make piecrust pastry

Cut 8 tablespoons (1 stick) of BUTTER into cubes and chill for 10 minutes, along with scant 1½ cups of ALL-PURPOSE FLOUR and a glass of COLD WATER—the cooler everything is, the better.

Add the cubes of butter to the flour and rub in with the tips of your fingers until it resembles bread crumbs. This should take 5 minutes. Resist rubbing with your palms, as this will get the mixture too warm. Once good and crumbly, add a splash of cold water and quickly knead to bring together. Add another splash if needs be. Once well bound, wrap tightly in cling wrap and put back in the refrigerator for another 10 minutes.

Rolling out

Flour a clean work surface and a rolling pin—a wine bottle will suffice in desperate circumstances. Flatten the pastry into a rough circle and, starting in the middle, roll away from you. Rotate by about a quarter (there's no need to flip it over if you keep turning it) and roll again. Keep rolling and turning, rolling and turning, until a uniform thickness of about ¼ inch. Be bold—you are the boss of the pastry. Turn it with authority and confidence. If you prod and poke at it then it will rebel.

Lining your pan

Get a 10-inch tart pan. Lay the rolling pin near the edge of the rolled pastry closest to you and fold the bottom edge over it. Roll away from you, rolling the pastry around the pin. Put the tart pan where the pastry was and roll the pastry back over. Carefully work around the pan, pushing the pastry into the edges. Trim off any excess, leaving a lip around the edge. Prick all over with a fork and put in the refrigerator for half an hour.

Surfing the stumbling blocks

TART—For something a bit sharper, add a little lemon zest to the pastry. Or try using an egg yolk to bind the pastry rather than some of the water for a richer crust.

TWEAK—Add ½ cup of confectioners' sugar to the flour for a sweeter version. Swap a tablespoon of the flour for one of unsweetened cocoa powder to give you a chocolate pastry.

Cooking

Preheat the oven to 350°F. Line the pastry with a sheet of parchment paper and tip in a handful of dried chickpeas or something similar—something to weigh it down and stop it from collapsing. Bake in the oven for 20 minutes. Remove from the oven and tip out the chickpeas (save them for next time). Beat a little egg and brush the pastry. Return to the oven for 5 minutes. Done. This is known as "blind baking." From here you can fill the shell with whatever you choose, or freeze it for another time.

Things to bear in mind:
• Until you come to cook the pastry, keep it as cold as you possibly can.
• Be careful with the water you add. A too-wet pastry will crack more easily and will be tricky to roll out.

#pastry

Surfing the stumbling blocks

Onion and anchovy tart

The success of this dish lies in the long, slow cooking of the onions. Don't be shy with the butter, either.

Serves 8

1 x basic piecrust pastry recipe
  (p.178), or 10 ounces ready-
  made piecrust pastry
4 tablespoons butter
6 onions, peeled and
  finely sliced
salt and pepper
2 eggs
⅓ cup cream
scant 1 cup grated Gruyère or
  cheddar cheese
a can of salted anchovy fillets

Blind bake the pastry following the method explained on p.179. Meanwhile, melt the butter over low heat and add the onions. Season with salt and pepper, cover, and gently cook for an hour, stirring now and then.

Preheat the oven to 350°F. Let the onions cool a little. Beat together the eggs and cream and stir into the onions along with the cheese. Season with salt and pepper and pour into the tart shell. Lay the anchovies over the top in whatever pattern you fancy and cook in the preheated oven for 30 minutes.

Cool for 10 minutes before serving, or serve cold.

#oniontart

Shortbread

TART—Crushed fennel seeds are delicious in shortbread cookies, giving them a little more oomph.

While shortbread follows the same 2-parts-dry-to-1-part-butter principle on the previous pages, you need soft butter, not cold. The recipe is simple and old-fashioned and I rather love it for that. It takes next to no time, and how nifty is it to have a little tin of cookies to take to work with you once finished?

Makes about 30 cookies

¾ cup sugar
scant 1 cup softened butter
1¾ cups all-purpose flour
½ teaspoon salt

Beat the butter and sugar together until pale and fluffy. Sift in the flour and salt and stir until fully combined.

Line a baking pan with parchment paper and lightly butter. Press in the dough and lightly flatten with a rolling pin to about ½ inch thick. Chill in the refrigerator for half an hour.

Preheat the oven to 300°F and bake for an hour. Remove and cool for 5 minutes, before cutting into your preferred shape and leaving on a cooling rack until completely cool. Store in an airtight container. It should keep for a couple of weeks.

#shortbread

A cheese soufflé

Unlike a poached egg, for a soufflé you ideally want eggs that are about a week old. That way the whites whisk better and make a lighter soufflé. The freshest eggs tend to have three weeks shelf life, so just get eggs with a "best before" date within two weeks. Make sure they're at room temperature. Other than that, all you need is a little attention to detail. Just remember that you are aiming at something light, therefore the more air you can create and keep in the soufflé, the better.

Serves 4

1½ tablespoons butter
1 tablespoon grated Parmesan
⅔ cup whole milk
1 tablespoon all-purpose flour
½ cup grated Gruyère or cheddar cheese
a pinch of cayenne (optional)
salt and pepper
2 large eggs, at room temperature
1 egg white

Grease four individual ramekins with half the butter, using upward strokes. This sounds irredeemably finicky but it helps the soufflés to rise. Put a little Parmesan in each ramekin and roll them around to coat the sides evenly. Place in the refrigerator while you make the white sauce.

Preheat the oven to 425°F. Warm the milk in a small pan until almost boiling. In a separate pan, melt the remaining butter and stir in the flour. Cook for a couple of minutes, stirring regularly, before slowly pouring in the warm milk, stirring all the while until thickened. Add the Gruyère or cheddar cheese and cayenne, if using, then season with salt and pepper, turn the heat right down, and let cook very gently for 10 minutes or so.

Let the white sauce cool for a few minutes. Separate the eggs, putting the whites (plus the extra white) in a large, clean bowl. Tip the cooled white sauce into another bowl and stir through the egg yolks until smooth and glossy. You can do all this ahead, should you want to.

Whisk the egg whites until stiff—they should sit in stiff peaks. Beat a spoonful of the egg whites into the white sauce to loosen it a little, then carefully fold through the remaining whites. Remember, you're trying to keep all that air you beat into the whites. Gently spoon the mixture into the prepared ramekins to about ½ inch from the top.

Carefully place the ramekins on a cookie sheet and slide onto the middle shelf of the oven. Close the door softly. Turn the heat straight down to 375°F. Leave for 15 minutes, resisting the temptation to open the oven door to check their progress. Serve immediately.

#soufflé

Tip To make a smoked haddock soufflé, add 5 ounces undyed smoked haddock to the milk when you warm it and poach gently for 10 minutes. Remove and cool while you make the white sauce. Flake the fish and stir through the white sauce along with the cheese and proceed as before.

Surfing the stumbling blocks

Lemon and thyme soufflé

This is a bit of a cheat, using store-bought lemon curd, but really, who's going to know?

Serves 4

1 tablespoon softened butter, for greasing
1 tablespoon all-purpose flour
2 large eggs
1 egg white
4 tablespoons lemon curd
½ teaspoon minced thyme leaves
confectioners' sugar, for dusting

Preheat the oven to 425°F.

Grease four individual ramekins with butter in an upward motion and dust with flour. Place in the refrigerator.

Separate the eggs, putting the whites (plus the extra white) in a large, clean bowl. Beat the yolks with the lemon curd and thyme in a separate large bowl. Whisk the egg whites until they form stiff peaks. Gently fold the beaten egg whites through the curd, taking care not to knock out any air. Spoon the mixture into the chilled ramekins to about three-quarters full.

Carefully put on a baking sheet and slide into the oven. Turn down to 375°F and leave for 15 minutes. Avoid peeking. Remove, dust with confectioners' sugar, and serve immediately.

#lemonsouffle

Meringues

Meringues are a useful thing to know how to bake, particularly when you're making things like mayonnaise (p.164), which require yolks but no whites. They're also very easy to make, and freeze well.

How to make meringues
Preheat the oven to 275°F, and line a baking sheet with a sheet of parchment paper. Lightly rub with SUNFLOWER OIL. Whisk 4 EGG WHITES in a clean bowl until they reach the soft peak stage—i.e. when an upward flourish with the whisk causes the whites to sit in peaks. Now whisk in 1 cup of SUPERFINE SUGAR, a spoonful at a time, until thick and glossy and you can hold the bowl upside down over your head. Spoon the mixture into 6–8 pieces onto the baking sheet, leaving a little space in between each. Put on a low shelf of the oven and bake for 1 hour. Turn the oven off, leaving the door ajar and the meringues in there until the oven is completely cool. The finished meringues will keep in an airtight container for a few weeks, or in the freezer for a couple of months.

#meringues

Boozy blackberry Eton mess

Serves 4

1 cup blackberries, plus extra for serving
1/3 cup crème de cassis
1 tablespoon confectioners' sugar
1 heaping cup heavy cream
a handful of meringues

Blend the blackberries with the crème de cassis and confectioners' sugar. Pass through a strainer and set aside.
Pour the heavy cream into a bowl and whip until it forms soft peaks. Crush the meringues into the cream, fold through the blackberry sauce, and serve topped with a scattering of whole blackberries.

#etonmess

Strawberry and elderflower pavlova

One of the best summer desserts, and so easy to make, too.

Serves 8

a little sunflower oil
4 egg whites
1 cup superfine sugar
1 heaping cup heavy cream
¼ cup elderflower syrup
2¾ cups strawberries, hulled
  and halved
confectioners' sugar, for dusting
  (optional)

Preheat the oven to 275°F. Line a baking sheet with parchment paper and brush with a little oil. Now whisk the egg whites until they form stiff peaks, before whisking in the sugar, a little at a time. The mixture should be glossy and thick. Carefully spoon this onto the baking sheet and fashion into something approaching a circle. Bake in the oven for 1½ hours. Turn the oven off and leave the meringue inside until the oven is completely cold.

Whip the cream with the elderflower syrup until it forms soft peaks, and dollop on top of the meringue. Dot with the strawberries and dust with a little confectioners' sugar, if you fancy.

#pavlova

Glossary

Aioli—Garlic mayonnaise.
Barberries—Small red fruits. They're full of vitamin C but incredibly sharp, adding a lovely acidic edge to dishes.
Bean sprouts—Asian edibles that come from mung beans. Delicious raw or stir-fried.
Buttermilk—A slightly sour and thick milk.
Carpaccio—Very thin slices of raw beef.
Cardamom—Small green pods used in Indian cooking.
Chapatti—Indian flatbread, a less pillowy version of naan, essentially.
Cornichons—Small, crunchy pickled gherkins.
Enoki—Long, thin, white mushrooms used predominantly in Asian cuisine. They taste, oddly enough, like chestnut honey.
Fish sauce—Don't smell it. It's not pleasant, but a little added to an Asian broth or dressing adds incredible depth and savor.
Goat curd—Goat-milk yogurt with the whey drained out of it—it's like the creamiest, smoothest, tangiest goat cheese you've ever tasted.
Gremolata—A combination of chopped parsley, garlic, and lemon zest, traditionally served with *ossobuco* (p.42).
Harissa—A north African chili paste. It's amazingly versatile, and can work in anything that benefits from a chili, smoky undertone.
Jerusalem artichoke—Looks like a nobbly little potato. Tastes like an artichoke. Makes you fart. What's not to love?
Kale—A kind of cabbage.
Kielbasa—An East European sausage, often smoked.
Lovage—A herb that looks like overgrown parsley and tastes like strong celery.
Marsala—A fortified wine from Sicily, quite similar to port, as these things go.
Mirin—Japanese rice wine.
Ossobuco—A northern Italian dish made with veal shank.
Paneer—A fresh (i.e. unaged) cheese from India. Good for cooking with as it doesn't melt.
Pea shoots—Also known as pea tops, they are the leaves from a pea plant and you can find them in most supermarkets these days. Once you've tried them there's no going back—they're delicious.
Pilau, pulao, pilaff, pilaf, etc—Rice dish with variations across the globe, but essentially it's rice (or another grain) browned in oil and cooked in a broth.

Polenta—Dried and ground corn, basically (also known as cornmeal), polenta is a bit of an acquired taste, but when cooked with enough butter and Parmesan is delicious. It also makes a good flour replacement in baking—River Café has an awesome recipe for lemon polenta cake.

Raita—A yogurt accompaniment for Indian food. Try a breakfast raita of bananas, honey, almonds, raisins, and cardamom.

Ramekin – A small, round dish. The sort of thing you often get a crème brûlée in.

Ras el hanout—A North African spice blend. *Ras el hanout* literally means "top of the shop," meaning it's a blend of all the best spices in the store. It is also, supposedly, an aphrodisiac. But what isn't these days?

Remoulade—A mayonnaise-based condiment, most usually found clinging to raw, grated celery root with a ton of mustard.

Rillettes—A coarse pâté usually made with very slow-cooked pork or duck.

Sauté pan—Basically a frying pan with high sides. Really useful for sauces and risottos.

Shallot—Little onions, essentially. They are sweeter and less pungent than their more overgrown cousins, and are useful when you want only the most subtle whiff of allium.

Short ribs—Short ribs are chunky beef ribs and, when you first try them, you'll wonder where they've been all your life.

Skate—a flat fish.

Star anise—An anise flavored and star-shaped spice used frequently in Asian cuisine.

Sweat—Slightly odd but actually quite logical expression for very gently cooking vegetables over low heat until soft but not brown.

Szechuan pepper—The pith from a tiny Asian fruit. Confusingly, not in any way related to black pepper.

Tahini—Sesame paste, used mostly in Middle Eastern and North African cooking. Mostly.

Taleggio—A soft and tangy Italian cheese.

Turmeric—A dried spice used in Asian and Middle Eastern cooking.

Zabaglione—A dessert made with egg yolks, sugar, and some kind of booze—usually Marsala.

Index

A million thanks to:

Mom and Dad, for allowing their kitchen to be subjected to experimentation and mayhem so often over the years, and for being so wise, supportive, and kind. Sarah Randell, who gave me my first writing gig. Fiona Beckett, who keeps me on the straight and narrow and let me be a part of her *Ultimate Student Cookbook*.

Darren, Trench, Dodge, Swoz, Emilie, Sam, Alex, JP, Lydia, Eddie, and Jack, for putting up with me as a roommate and feeder over the years.

Ollie Thring, for being an endless source of entertainment and support while I wrote this book. Darina Allen and Eileen Buchanan, for being the best teachers a young cook could ask for. Jennifer Christie, for being a wonderful agent and friend, and Jane Graham Maw, for her ever-sage advice. Rachel Purnell for being my fairy godmother. Alex Franklin, Katie Harrison, and Nicole Karalekas, for their guidance. Bash Redford for his friendship and selfless help with everything. Rachel, Giles, and Stefan for their kind words.

Steven Joyce for the incredible photographs and for making the shoots such fun.

The team at Quadrille Books: my editor Simon Davis for putting the words in the right order and being so calm when I was panicking; Nikki Davidson for making it look so fantastic, and Jane O'Shea and Clare Lattin for their enthusiasm and faith in me.

And finally to everyone else who's helped along the way. Blog readers, supper-club guests, recipe testers, and tweeters—I couldn't have written this without you.

Much love,
James.